PENGUIN BOOKS

CALM MOTHER, CALM CHILD

Paul Wilson thrives in several high-stress worlds: successful businessman, strategic consultant to major corporations, father to a teenager and two young children, and director of a hospital and medical research foundation.

To thrive in these worlds, he has mastered the secrets of calm. His first book, *The Calm Technique*, is widely acknowledged as one of the most influential books in the genre. His second, *The Big Book of Calm*, has been translated into twenty languages. His third, *The Little Book of Calm*, has spent more than two years at the top of the bestseller lists, with sales of over three million copies. The success continues with *Calm at Work*, *Calm for Life* and *Calm Mother, Calm Child*.

You can contact the author at www.calmcentre.com

If you would like to know how calm can transform your workplace, go to www.calmatwork.com

Calm Mother, Calm Child

PAUL WILSON
WITH TANIA WILSON

PENGUIN BOOKS

PENGUIN BOOKS

Published by the Penguin Group
Penguin Books Ltd, 80 Strand, London WC2R 0RL, England
Penguin Putnam Inc., 375 Hudson Street, New York, New York 10014, USA
Penguin Books Australia Ltd, 250 Camberwell Road, Camberwell, Victoria 3124, Australia
Penguin Books Canada Ltd, 10 Alcorn Avenue, Toronto, Ontario, Canada M4V 3B2
Penguin Books India (P) Ltd, 11 Community Centre, Panchsheel Park, New Delhi – 110 017, India
Penguin Books (NZ) Ltd, Cnr Rosedale and Airborne Roads, Albany, Auckland, New Zealand
Penguin Books (South Africa) (Pty) Ltd, 24 Sturdee Avenue, Rosebank 2196, South Africa

Penguin Books Ltd, Registered Offices: 80 Strand, London WC2R 0RL, England

www.penguin.com

First published in Australia by Penguin 2001
First published in Great Britain in Penguin Books 2002

2

Set in Sabon
Printed in England by Clays Ltd, St Ives plc

Contents

Before the calm

Parenthood can be one of life's greatest joys. As Dostoevsky said, 'The soul is healed by being with children.'

But even Dostoevsky would have to admit that one of the most stressful jobs in the world is being a parent. When you're in the thick of it, the tensions of parenthood seem more formidable than anything experienced in traffic, the workplace or the classroom.

Why is being a parent such a stressful job?

Because underpinning these pressures is the feeling that there is no escape. You can't just walk away, go out for a movie or join your friends in the bar. If you have a crying baby or a problem child, *you* have to deal with the situation.

Calm Mother, Calm Child does more than help you deal with the stress of being a parent. This book will help bring a little calm to your life so you can discover, or continue to enjoy, the pleasures of being with your child.

There was some shaking of heads when we settled on the title *Calm Mother, Calm Child*. What about *Calm Parent, Calm Child*? After all, in this day and age, such inclusiveness recognises the shared responsibilities of mother and father in the parenting process.

I agree. But very early in our research it became clear that the issues and concerns that relate to mothers and fathers of young children are usually so different they would not sit comfortably in the same book.

We learnt that, overwhelmingly, it is mothers who believe they are most pressured by parenthood, especially in those early years – the latter stages of pregnancy, until the child is 12 to 18 months, and sometimes continuing for another year or two. Naturally there will be stressful periods that follow this – school years and adolescence introduce tensions into even the calmest families. Even though the focus of *Calm Mother, Calm Child* is on younger children, the principles involved often apply to older ones as well.

We also learnt that when two people share the responsibilities of looking after a child, it is usually one who ends up carrying the burden – both physically and emotionally – regardless of the intentions of the parties concerned. More often than not, that person is the mother.

And, most interesting of all, we learnt that mothers and fathers often respond quite differently in the ways they try to deal with the pressures of parenthood. Fathers tend to seek a solution to their 'problem', while mothers tend to work on the way they feel about it. (Yes, this is a generalisation; each person is, of course, an individual.)

However, at the risk of overlooking a few uniquely father-related needs, this book focuses on the issues raised by mothers, especially new mothers.

With all this emphasis on mothers and children, you may well ask, 'What does Paul Wilson know about being a calm mother?'

I certainly know about the 'calm' part. The calm practices I encourage and write about are already being used by hundreds of thousands of mothers around the world.

As for the 'mother' part, it is not sufficient that I spent a number of years as a solo parent trying to fathom this role. So the maternal understandings that shape the pages that follow come from mothers themselves – those who are, or have been, experiencing the pressures of this role.

The research approach we adopted for *Calm Mother, Calm Child* differed from that of my other books. Instead of relying on professional or academic researchers, we sought advice from child-care experts or psychologists who also happened to be mothers of babies or young children. We could therefore be sure that the concerns and experiences of parenthood were fresh in their minds.

Through the networks of these researchers and those of my collaborator, Tania, we have been able to interview, discuss and explore the effectiveness of our recommendations with a great many mothers and fathers of young children over the past three years.

Calm Mother, Calm Child is not intended to be the definitive work on raising children. Its purpose is to be a comfort to you in those moments when you really feel the pressure of parenthood.

Use *Calm Mother, Calm Child* as a guide. Use it as a handy escape from the pressures of the everyday. Use it as a way of gaining more pleasure from your role as a parent.

And, most important of all, use it often to stay calm.

chapter one

Starting point

Children are natural mimics who

act like their parents despite every effort

to teach them good manners.

Anonymous

The pleasure of calm

The purpose of *Calm Mother, Calm Child* is to spread calm. So let's start at the end result – the calm feeling or state you intend to create or restore.

Just for a moment, think of one joyous, uplifting experience that relates to your role as a parent. Just one calm, satisfying moment from your past, or one you'd love to experience in the future.

Think back now . . . Can you bring to mind a time when you were utterly calm, or a time when you held your infant in your arms, simply enjoying the moment? Feeling safe, secure and contented. You may not have thought about it at the time, but you were experiencing a calm, pleasurable feeling – intensely satisfying, and peaceful at the same time.

This feeling is your starting point. It is the benchmark feeling you refer back to as you become more and more calm.

There are all sorts of sentimental phrases people use to describe the experience you've just recalled. Essentially, though, it is a combination of two things: calm and rapport.

'Calm' we can understand, but 'rapport' isn't a word normally associated with the parent–baby relationship.

Some years ago, researchers from the Calm Centre conducted a range of experiments involving the brainwave activity of people as they experienced deep states of relaxation, such as during massage or meditation. Of particular interest were our observations of a breast-feeding mother. Repeatedly, the mother's brainwave activity displayed the same relaxed patterns we had recorded from other people in deep meditation. The thought of breastfeeding as a form of meditation was not something we'd considered, but there was no surprise that it could be a deeply relaxing experience.

What we did find surprising was the pattern recorded by the child she was nursing. The baby's brainwave activity was almost identical to that of the mother. When either mother or baby shifted out of their relaxed state – say when the baby had wind, or the mother was distracted – the brainwave pattern of the other would alter to mirror this change.

To those involved in the experiment, it was more than a demonstration of emotional rapport, it was a graphic confirmation of a phenomenon many of us instinctively knew to be true: **When two people are in a state of rapport, their emotions tend to work in parallel. If one is relaxed, the other relaxes; if one is tense, the other becomes tense.**

You know from your own experience how easy it is for emotional states to be transferred from one person to another. How many times have you been in a group of relaxed people when an anxious person barges in and, before you know it, everyone is stressed out? Fortunately the opposite of this rule also applies: a calm person spreads calm.

This simple understanding of the transfer of calm emotional states is the foundation for *Calm Mother, Calm Child*. **When you maintain the calm within yourself then, more often than not, this calm can be passed onto your child.**

Of course, it won't always work this way. Sometimes illness or discontent in your child overwhelms whatever attempts you make. However, in spite of these impediments, the fact remains that if you can maintain the calm within yourself, it can generally be passed onto your child and those around you.

Bring back the feeling of calm

Recall what it feels like, *or would feel like*, for both you and your baby to be completely relaxed and at ease.

- Run a warm bath. Light a candle and turn off the lights.
- Drape a warm face towel over your face as you sink down into the tub.
- Tell yourself you have all the time in the world.
- Listen to your relaxed breathing as you forget the world outside.
- Imagine you are holding your infant in your arms, enjoying being in that moment, feeling safe, secure and that all is well in the world.
- *Remember this feeling.* Refer back to it often – not only for your own pleasure, but so that you can impart some of it to your baby in the future.

The side effects of parenthood

There's no escaping the fact that, along with all the joys of parenthood, there may be a few unsettling side effects.

Remember what life was like before your baby? You probably felt in control then. You felt you knew how to set goals and achieve them – more or less. You felt you were a competent person who managed to deal with difficulties and even crises – more or less.

You probably had a relationship then, too. Let's say your relationship with your partner was fulfilling – more or less. You enjoyed a few common interests and pursuits. You liked to discuss issues of the day with each other and friends over dinner and a glass of wine. You went to the movies. You had a sex life.

And, even though you probably didn't appreciate it then, you had spare time. You read books and newspapers. You took time out for a coffee, and maybe went for a walk each day.

Then it all changed.

Ironically, parents often find the stresses that accompany the arrival of a new baby are entirely predictable. You knew to expect broken sleep, fatigue, constant demands on your time, crying, relationship tensions and so on. You just weren't quite prepared for it.

You're not alone. All these strains are normal and, believe it or not, temporary. Every new mother feels under pressure at one stage or another, perhaps many times a day. It's not ideal and it may not even be necessary, but it is normal. Accepting this fact is the first step towards bringing peace and calm to your life.

The second step is identifying the reasons you feel stressed so you can take steps to overcome them.

At the top of the list are issues that relate to **life circumstances, uncertainty, time,** the level of **control** you feel you have over what's going on and the **pressures** you place on yourself.

Life circumstances

Some people live in comfortable surroundings, yet find physical stresses are one of the primary causes of discomfort in their lives. These can range from illness or uncomfortable shoes, to environmental conditions such as noise, cold or dust. However, the most prominent one is more clandestine. It's sleep disturbance.

Even with the best plans, a new baby means learning to live with broken sleep.

It's a physiological fact that sleep deprivation does peculiar things to a person. If you miss two hours of sleep, your IQ will fall measurably (until you catch up). Miss out on consecutive nights and your reaction time is impaired. Three consecutive days and your immune system weakens. And if you're forced to continue this for a week or longer, watch out!

Combine this with physical fatigue, which many new mothers experience, and you have a particularly stressful cocktail.

Uncertainty

In the early days, new parents are often distressed because they don't know why their baby is crying. Is it illness? Colic? Wind? Or is it nothing to worry about?

Until you are familiar with your baby's signals and behaviour, this uncertainty can be disturbing.

And, although the uncertainty may change in nature, it often continues as your child grows older. What is the cause of your two-year-old's whimpering? Why do they react the way they do?

Time

Time is blamed for so many of the pressures that arise during any person's working day. With parents of young children, these pressures seem even more pronounced.

Demands come from all directions – the housework is mounting, there's shopping to do, and there are nowhere near enough hours in the day. At times it may seem these pressures will never ease.

Control

The less control you exert over any given situation, the more likely you are to suffer a degree of stress, fear or anxiety.

This is also why you feel stressed and frustrated when you have to perform monotonous, repetitive tasks, or when you feel you lack choices in what you do. (Sometimes it's even stressful when you feel you have too many choices.)

However, the most frustrating times of all arise from managing small children. When you cannot dictate behaviour, such as with small children, or how events should unfold, you can only respond to them. This makes you feel that the situation is in control of you rather than the other way around.

The only thing in life you can really control is yourself – your actions, attitudes and perceptions. Bring them into line and you'll start to *feel* that you're in control.

Self-pressure

By far the greatest cause of unrest comes not from any of the above areas, but from inside your head: what you think or feel, your habits and how you react to events.

The comfort of knowing this is realising that the solutions reside in the same place – within you.

Take your time

To remove some of the perceived time pressures that accompany the stage of life you are experiencing, repeat these words to yourself – often:

'I have all the time in the world.'

Say it to yourself now. Hear the words. Hear yourself saying them, slowly, at least three times.

Have you begun to notice how just a few simple words have started to make you feel freer already?

Decide to be calm

Just for a moment, imagine your only responsibility in life is not how your child feels or how your partner feels, but how *you* feel. (There is no selfishness in this because it's only happening in your imagination.)

Sure, there's a lot going on right now – change, new demands and shifting emotions – but you have only this one responsibility: how you feel and how you cope.

While it is perfectly natural to experience the pressures, emotions and tensions that accompany being a parent, it's a waste of time trying to think you can control them. **You cannot control these factors. All you have real control over is how you experience them, or how you feel.**

And you *can* feel calm.

Once you learn how to feel calm, at will, you can begin to reduce the impact of life's inevitable ups and downs. You'll:

- feel more alive, healthier and happier
- be more positive and focused
- have a greater capacity to cope
- be more tolerant
- be open to appreciate the joys of your child
- be more energetic and alert
- appreciate life more

Imagine how relieved you'll feel once you have a range of simple, pleasurable ways to deal with the stresses of parenthood. And imagine the calming effect this will have on other people's lives.

Remember, though, **being calm is not an outcome but a process**. There will be days when the techniques that follow will work exactly as you imagined, and other times they might bring only minimal relief. Once you have chosen a few as your routine, there is no need to evaluate their effectiveness – just enjoy them for what they are. They aren't tasks you need to accomplish so much as little indulgences and escapes in your day.

So now you have an easy choice to make. When it comes to the aspects of life that cause you stress, you can either:

- change the circumstances that cause you stress, or
- change the way you look at them.

While it can be difficult to change physical circumstances or long-standing habits and attitudes, you *can* change the way they affect you. And you'll find it progressively easier as you move through this book.

That's only the beginning of your choices. Here's another: **choose to become calm**.

Make the decision – now – and you've already commenced the process of becoming a more relaxed person. It is happening of its own accord. You may not be fully aware of it yet, but the calm change has already begun.

All it took was a decision. Are you starting to feel more relaxed?

chapter two

Calm for you

There is no joy but calm.

Tennyson, THE LOTUS EATERS

Thinking about yourself

How do you feel?

While much of what you will read in the second half of this book is devoted to ways you can bring calm to your child, it's really how *you* feel that will make the difference.

This emphasis on how you feel is not selfishness. Feeling strong and positive within yourself is as beneficial for your child's wellbeing as for your own. It is difficult to calm a child if you're feeling uptight yourself. Conversely, your child will be much more receptive to your calming efforts if your approach is calm.

So the aim of this chapter is to explore a number of pleasant ways to add a little calm to your day. Note that word – 'pleasant'. Pleasure and calm are wonderful companions. Have you ever noticed how you start to relax when you're feeling good?

What follows is going to help you feel good. And you will feel much better if you keep four important principles in mind:

1. You are an individual

Just like your child, you are a unique being. There is no-one else in the universe quite like you. No-one's problems are exactly the same as yours. No-one's child is exactly like yours. And, deep down, no-one knows better than you what is best for you.

The calming techniques or strategies that work best for one person may not be the ones that work best for you, and vice versa. With this book, trust your instincts. There should be no sense of failure if some strategies do not appeal. If just one of the techniques that follow helps you to feel more calm and relaxed in your role as a parent, this book will have been well worth the read.

2. There's no hurry

You have all the time in the world to become a calmer person. Yes, all the time in the world. Repeat these words to yourself – often – and you'll remove many of the time pressures that keep creeping up on you as you deal with life as a new mother.

3. You don't have to be perfect

Many first-time parents are weighed down by the belief that only perfection is good enough when it comes to the way they approach their responsibilities: the perfectly maintained child in the perfectly maintained household. You might expect this to be a concern of 'perfectionists' (excuse the stereotype), but our research indicates that this is also the concern of many new mothers who are fresh out of the workplace.

Sometimes women who have been capable, dependable employees or managers try to apply the same professional zeal to motherhood. They quickly discover that motherhood involves a vastly different dynamic.

For a start, babies have no concept of weekends, holidays or time off. Nor do they take kindly to adopting the routine that most suits you. And they don't give pay rises or acknowledge a job well done. Equally as frustrating is the fact that babies are not goal oriented – or even process oriented. They just *are*. Regardless of your best efforts, your child will develop at his or her own pace.

4. You deserve it

You are a unique being whose purpose in life, among other things, is to be happy and enjoy it. You deserve it. The only period in your existence that you can be absolutely sure of is now – this very moment. If you can find fulfilment and satisfaction in this moment, both as an individual and as a parent, you will lead a happy, contented life. And if you fret about the past or worry too much about the future you will limit this potential.

Or you could look at it from another point of view.

By being a parent, you are bringing a child into *your* world. This carries a great responsibility. The very best gift you can give your child is the ability to enjoy life, to find fulfilment and satisfaction in every moment he or she experiences. And the most effective way to impart that understanding is to live it yourself.

Now it's time to start turning your attention to yourself – not to analyse how you feel or how you're coping, but to explore ways of helping yourself feel better and more fulfilled.

It is easy for a new parent to become so occupied with the mundane that they overlook their own basic needs. This can lead to stress, feeling overwhelmed, or even depression.

Devote just a few minutes each day to yourself, and you'll effect a significant change in how you think and feel. Even though it may seem like you have chores and duties for every waking moment, make an effort to rediscover some of the activities you used to enjoy before you were a mother. Or take up something new and challenging – learn a new skill, listen to a self-help tape, take a yoga class.

The important thing is not what you do, but that you do it for yourself. So *you* will get the enjoyment out it. So *you* will grow as an individual. So *you* will get more out of this role that takes up so much of your day.

Time for you

If you've read any of my earlier books, such as *Calm for Life* and *The Calm Technique*, you will be acquainted with an enriching practice that I encourage everyone to make part of their life. I call it Me Time.

In this day and age, most people allow themselves very little self time – a brief period when they take time out and do absolutely nothing but dwell on what good company they can be.

When you have a young child in the house, this time becomes even rarer, and seems impossible. You probably think that if you did have a free hour, there would be so many more 'productive' things you could do – catch up with your friends, read a newspaper or watch a TV program.

Ironically, Me Time is a much more productive use of your time. By relaxing and restoring order to your thoughts and physiology, you will be able to approach the other activities of your day with increased energy, application and enjoyment.

Me Time requires no effort or training. It's a time that has no inherent purpose other than simply being. Being yourself. Being relaxed. Being calm. Being restored.

It will allow you to escape the pressures and responsibilities of your day – without structure, without a sense of guilt. If you need an excuse, tell yourself it will help you become a better parent or partner. (It will.)

Me Time

Take 20–30 minutes each day just to be with yourself. The object of this time is to do nothing. Just be. In order to do this you might choose to:

- sit under a tree
- sit in a dark corner of your living room
- meditate

Remember, this is *your* time – a time of indulgence when you can forget your responsibilities, be yourself and simply relax.

Me Time is at its most powerful when it is a routine. It is particularly important for those whirlwind times after the birth of a new baby, when you begin to think that you are continually at the beck and call of another party and have no real life of your own.

Pamper Time

Add a touch of pampering to Me Time, and you will feel truly indulged. Pamper Time is meant to remind you of those carefree, possibly even luxurious moments you may have enjoyed when you were not on call 24 hours a day.

The practice of pampering yourself, and just yourself, works best when you firmly acknowledge that you deserve it. Consider it a reward for a job well done – one that earns no direct thanks or rewards in its own right – for raising a child.

Becoming calm and relaxed is one of the few aspects of life that works better the easier you take it. The better you feel, the more 'feel-good' neuro-chemicals your brain produces, and the more capable you are of enjoying life and being relaxed.

One of the best examples of this is massage. You could view massage as an expensive indulgence, something for athletes or the idle rich, or you could see it for its long-term therapeutic benefits. For the cost of a candle-lit dinner, you not only get an hour of physical pleasure, you also enjoy a unique combination of deep relaxation and energy – tingling skin, loose muscles and a peace-filled mind. And unlike a candle-lit dinner, the relaxing benefits of a massage continue throughout the week.

Once you let your imagination loose on the following exercise, it's amazing the number of pampering add-ons you'll think of.

Pamper Time

Pamper Time is meant to remind you of those carefree moments when you were not on call 24 hours a day. Here are a few possibilities:

- Treat yourself to a massage, facial or an hour in a flotation tank.
- Take a long hot bath using your favourite essential oils or bath salts.
- Take yourself off for an hour and indulge in a delicious lunch. For an extra measure of indulgence, consider doing this solo.
- Go to the movies.
- Get your hair done or have a manicure.

Make a list of appealing activities and paste it onto your bathroom mirror to constantly remind yourself of them.

Solo massage

While massage in its traditional styles is an ideal pampering tool, its limitation is that it requires the involvement of another party.

Or does it?

When you think about it, no-one is better equipped to massage away your aches and stresses than the person who experiences them – you. After all, no-one knows better than you where the tender spots are, what feels uncomfortable and what feels right.

The purpose of self-massage is not to work your muscles but to occupy the senses so completely that your mind is stilled and your thoughts come to rest. The moment that happens you will become deeply relaxed.

Following are a few self-massaging techniques that will bring some of the calming, healing relief of massage without the involvement of another party. This is particularly useful during pregnancy, when your body is changing day by day.

Self-massage

- Take the phone off the hook.
- Mix together a blend of Vitamin E oil and a carrier oil such as sweet almond or apricot kernel.
- Go to a quiet place where you will not be disturbed. Remove your clothes and relax on a soft bath towel.
- Just listen to your breathing for a couple of minutes and become comfortable with your surroundings.
- Slowly oil your body, taking care to cover the surface of your tummy, legs, feet, arms, neck, face, shoulders – in fact, every place you can comfortably reach.
- Begin to massage each part of your body slowly and methodically. Concentrate your attention where your hands touch your body.
- Be conscious of what it feels like both through your hands and your body.
- Draw out this process slowly, methodically and calmly for 20–30 minutes.

An alternative to the massage technique opposite is to fill a bath with warm water, turn off the lights and listen to your relaxed breathing as your tension floats away. Make it even more indulgent by adding bath salts or essential oils, burning a candle and playing relaxing music in the background.

Face massage 1

If you've ever had a facial, you will have experienced the relaxed feelings that accompany light pressure on certain points around the face (a). You will recognise these acupressure points by feel, but experimentation will reveal their precise location. These points are:

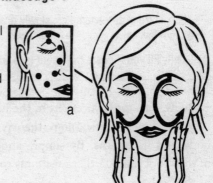

a

- just beneath the eyebrow
- above the eye socket
- where the eyebrow meets the nose
- beside your nose
- in line with your nostrils
- in the indent beneath your cheekbone
- at the top of your jaw muscle.

Massage outwards in a circular motion, as slowly and as sensually as you dare.

Face massage 2

Using the heels of your palms, slide your hands right around your head until they meet at the back.

Do this slowly, sensuously, with as much pressure as feels comfortable.

Once you have done it a number of times, your face will feel so relaxed that all it takes to set your skin tingling is the lightest brush of your fingertips.

Then, starting at the temples, slowly drag your fingers *down* to the point of your jaw.

Gently lift your fingers from your face and start again.

Now, let's move along from the head to the feet.

According to reflexology theory, the feet are mini maps of the body and its organs. By simply applying pressure to specific areas of this 'foot map', a therapist aims to relieve problems in other parts of the body.

Whatever the wider claims about the healing properties of reflexology, it does work wonders in the area of stress relief and relaxation. Massaging the feet stimulates thousands of nerve endings, which can clear neural pathways, facilitate deep relaxation and improve circulation. Better still, this is a treatment you can easily apply yourself.

The Foot Job

- Find a quiet, restful place and take a few minutes to soak your feet, or clean them with a warm, wet towel. Rub in a little moisturiser, body cream or a relaxing combination of essential oils.
- Massage each toe individually, then stretch. Rotate your foot one way, then the other.
- With your left hand, firmly hold the toes of your left foot. Make a fist with your right hand and press up from beneath – just behind the toes (a). Now squeeze. Repeat.
- Ensure your ankle is loose and relaxed. Move your foot from side to side.
- Use the lightest brush of your fingertips to sensitise the nerve endings in your feet – from ankles to toes, tops and bottoms of your feet.
- Repeat with your right foot.

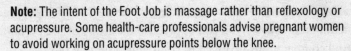

Note: The intent of the Foot Job is massage rather than reflexology or acupressure. Some health-care professionals advise pregnant women to avoid working on acupressure points below the knee.

The good oils

Aromatherapy must be one of the most written-about topics of the day. You may think it is a relatively new discovery, but it has been around in various forms for over 6000 years. Originally used in Chinese medicine, aromatherapy utilises pure, essential plant extracts to produce a range of physical and psychological effects.

The claims for aromatherapy are as diverse as they are extravagant. However, we now know that scents from certain essential oils have a real and measurable effect on the nervous system, most notably in the production of serotonin – the 'feel good' neuro-chemical.

If you experiment with essential oils, you will quickly discover a group that have powerful calming properties. This group includes lavender, ylang ylang, rose, orange blossom and chamomile. Others to consider are cedarwood, sandalwood, geranium, bergamot, neroli and patchouli.

So, how do you go about choosing the oils that are right for you?

The first question to resolve is simply what you want to achieve. Do you want to produce a calming ambience in your home? Do you want to compensate for the harmful effects of stress on your body? Or do you just want to feel more relaxed?

Each oil produces a slightly different effect. Used in combination, these effects vary slightly once again. And, when you take into account that each person is different – responding to various scents and stimuli in quite different ways – you can appreciate the scope of the permutations and combinations involved in combining essential oils.

The chart opposite outlines the characteristics of aromatherapy oils that are primarily used for their ability to calm, uplift and/or overcome the ill-effects of stress. (Many aromatherapists warn against using certain oils when you are pregnant. If you are pregnant, or if you suffer from hypertension or epilepsy, please consult a health-care professional before using *any* oils in a direct way.)

Use this list to determine those most suitable for you, then audition them: simply uncap the bottle and, keeping it some distance

from your nose, apply the scent test. Trust your instincts. Your nose
will guide you to the most suitable oils for you.

Essential oils

Oils	Calming	Uplifting	For overcoming stress	Avoid while pregnant
Basil	✓	✓		✓
Bay	✓			✓
Bergamot	✓	✓		
Cedarwood	✓			
Chamomile	✓		✓	
Cinnamon	✓			
Comfrey	✓			✓
Cypress	✓			
Frankincense	✓			
Geranium	✓	✓	✓	
Hyssop	✓			✓
Juniper	✓	✓		✓
Lavender	✓	✓	✓	
Marjoram	✓		✓	✓
Melissa	✓	✓	✓	✓
Neroli	✓			
Patchouli	✓			
Peppermint			✓	
Rose	✓			
Clary sage	✓			✓
Sandalwood	✓		✓	
Ylang ylang	✓			

Using two or three oils, experiment with different combinations to determine the effects they produce. There are many ways in which you can apply them.

For massage, add a few drops of the pure oils to a heavier (bland) massage oil such as apricot or jojoba.

For your bath, add about 10 drops to a steaming tub, turn down the lights or light a candle, and soak away your aches and worries.

Foot baths are also suited to aromatic oils. Add four or five drops to warm water and soak your feet. If your partner is willing, have him massage your feet as well.

Alternatively, add a few drops of oil to water in an oil burner, light a candle beneath it and let the oil weave its relaxing magic.

A calm attitude

Have you ever peered over a rocky ledge and shuddered at how far below the ground was? Being at the edge like that might be stressful in the extreme. But, if you were a passionate rock climber or abseiler, you might react to that same ledge in a completely different way.

The same view in both cases is a rocky escarpment, but two totally different reactions to it are possible. On one hand, terror; on the other, excitement. Because it's not so much the stressor that dictates how you feel, it's the way you react to it.

Be calm by choice

The moment you realise you have choices, you will notice how you automatically begin to feel more relaxed and in control.

If you tell yourself, 'I must wash all my baby's bedclothes by noon,' you'll feel resentful and pressured. However, if you were to say, 'I can launder my baby's bedclothes, or I can take an hour for lunch at the bistro,' you will feel more comfortable if you choose to do that laundry.

Why? Because you believed you had the choice.

When it comes to being calm and feeling good about what you have to do, you have choices. It may be difficult to accept this when you're feeling stressed or if you feel trapped in a particular routine, but these choices do exist.

You have the power to be happy or unhappy, to be content or depressed, to be loved or unloved, to be tense or calm. Sometimes it takes a bit of effort or creativity to realise these choices exist, but it's worth looking for them.

To make it easier as time goes along, it helps to make a little game of recognising the choices. This is also an exercise in positive thinking. After you've done it a few times, it will start to become second nature.

Your choices

You can worry about all the work that's piling up as you 'waste' time reading a book.	*or*	You can relax and enjoy the calm you are experiencing right now.
You can bemoan the fact that your childless friends are off to the movies without you.	*or*	You can relax and enjoy the unique, precious relationship you have with your child.
You can resent the responsibility that parenthood has burdened you with.	*or*	You can relax and appreciate how privileged you are to be able to help another being thrive and prosper.
You can feel trapped by the incessant demands of a growing child.	*or*	You can relax and be thankful for the unquestioning love that you are given.

Making light work of it

In all aspects of life, you can choose the way you view things as well as the way you react to them. You can open the window and see a glorious world of love and compassion, or you can see a difficult world of greed and neglect. The choice is yours.

You may not be able to control the work you have to do, the circumstances of your life, the attitude of your partner or the temperament of your baby, but you *can* control the way you respond to them.

You can even transform the most unwelcome or mundane chore into a satisfying, meaningful and fulfilling activity.

If you try to do three things at once, you will discover that dividing your attention creates tension. However, concentrating your attention on only one thing has the opposite effect – it is calming, fulfilling and efficient.

Zen philosophy encourages concentration on the 'now', by occupying yourself completely in the moment. This concept applies not only to meditation and martial arts, but to all of life's activities. Being able to concentrate this way can turn an ordinary, everyday activity into a meditation. It increases efficiency and makes time fly.

When you dedicate yourself wholly to a task or an activity, immersing yourself in the detail and the execution of it, your attention is centred, your mind is filled with one thing, extraneous thoughts cease, and you begin to ease into a relaxed and efficient state.

Try this simple technique to help you learn to love and accept what you do, whatever you 'have' to do.

Concentrating on the 'now'

- Accept the task. Your challenge is to turn it into a creative and fulfilling activity.
- Occupy yourself wholly with the activity at hand. Whether you're preparing baby food, washing sheets, painting the bedroom or reading a magazine, commit to it as conscientiously and skilfully as you can.
- Ignore all external stimuli such as radio or conversation.
- Concentrate on each step of what you're doing. Immerse yourself in ▶

the detail. Be aware of every nuance of what is happening. Do it as thoroughly and gracefully as you can.

- Soon you will be totally absorbed by the activity. You will be accepting, calm and at peace.

Simple, isn't it? It's like making a meditation out of your everyday activities.

Turning negative into positive

Even the most subtle negative thoughts have a way of upsetting the flow of your day. Not only do they make you feel stressed and unable to cope, but they can have a detrimental effect on your physical and mental health. Yet, if you choose to, you can dispense with negative thoughts quite effortlessly.

If you ask most people how they would achieve this, they might immediately think of willpower – forcing these negative thoughts or feelings from their mind. This does not work. Willpower has very little influence over the way we think or feel.

The first step is to accept that you cannot directly dispense with negative thoughts. You cannot consciously force yourself *not* to think in a certain way; psychologically speaking, it's almost impossible. The only way to consciously change a thought is to substitute another. So, if you wish to dispense with negative thoughts or feelings, instead of trying to suppress them, simply substitute positive ones.

Say you're feeling depressed about the mountain of chores that's building up. There's no way you can force yourself to stop thinking about how far behind you're falling – these thoughts just sit there in the back of your mind, making you feel restless and tense.

Try this instead: rather than concentrate on all you still have to do, concentrate on how much you've already done. Alternatively, turn your thoughts to something you really enjoy and get pleasure out of – that last skiing holiday, a new coat you're thinking of buying, or the day you breezed through everything at work in a record time.

You don't eliminate negative feelings by trying to suppress them, but by substituting positive feelings. Instead of concentrating on what you still have to do, concentrate on what you've already achieved. Substitution is immeasurably more powerful than willpower in this respect.

To put this into a practical context, try the following technique. The more often you try it, the more enjoyable and habitual it will become.

A positive change

Look for a positive side to events or behaviours that you would normally consider to be purely negative. Humour can be a great way of doing this.

Say, for example, you are being kept awake by a restless baby. Instead of dwelling on your tiredness or irritability, tell yourself that you can now watch the late-night re-runs of *Gilligan's Island* without feeling lazy. (It doesn't compare with a full night's sleep, but it does add a hint of lightness to something that would normally be seen as an irritation.) ▶

Make a habit of looking for the upside, finding the good in what you do and what happens to you, and you'll soon be able to transform even the most difficult moods and situations into something positive. Then it will be much easier to remain calm.

Sometimes you might try to see the positive, but you are still convinced that things are too challenging at that particular time. Commonsense tells you that you've nothing to worry about; you may even have tried a few calming techniques that succeeded in calming your body down, yet you still feel restless.

Times like this do occur, for all of us. And, even though you can usually overcome this feeling by applying a combination of calming techniques, you may feel you lack the energy or the inclination to do so. Fortunately, there is one sure approach that will take effect in just a few minutes.

The calm pretence

Most stresses and anxieties that affect us are irrational. Usually they relate not to what is actually happening, but to what *might* happen or what others *might* think of us. These stem from the unconscious part of the mind.

It follows that if you could adjust your unconscious, you could remove many of these stresses and anxieties. But, as we've explored, you cannot will or force your unconscious to perform the way you want it to.

One of the most effective ways to influence this part of your mind is one you perfected yourself at a very tender age – the ability to pretend. Some of the most skilled psychotherapists utilise this device to overcome the barriers and intrusions of the conscious mind. You can use it to find peace and calm.

The Calm Role

Regardless of how you are feeling, or how you think you might seem to an onlooker, the Calm Role simply requires you to *act* like you're calm.

- Think what a calm person looks like. How do they move? How do they speak? What do they feel?
- Lower your voice.
- Slow down your speech to a tempo that feels a little slower than normal.
- Slow down your movements to a little slower than normal.
- Slow down your rate of breathing.
- Now, just pretend you're feeling as calm as you're acting in this role.
- Act like you're in complete control of the situation.
- Act as though everybody thinks you're this way all the time.

You'll be believing yourself in no time.

Calm affirmations

The single most influential force that shapes the way you think and feel is repetition.

When you were a child, it was how you learnt. Nowadays you call it 'practice'. You practise your golf swing over and over until the action becomes so ingrained in your consciousness that you never have to think about it. This repetition remains your key learning method throughout life. It's also the most effective way of directing your thoughts, feelings or behaviour into ways you desire them to be.

When you repeat a phrase to yourself it becomes ingrained in your unconscious and tends to become self-fulfilling. This kind of repetition is known as self-talk, internal dialogue, auto-suggestion or affirmation.

If you use it negatively ('I'll never master this program', 'I hate ironing', 'Housework is a pain'), you will never master the program, will always hate ironing, and will always find housework a pain.

If you use it positively ('This program is getting easier and easier to use', 'I'm a great ironer', 'I'm so fortunate to have work that is worthwhile'), you will feel more positive about the program, your ironing and housework.

At the Calm Centre we carried out a survey of people who use affirmation techniques and discovered there was a widespread dislike for the long-winded, pretentious affirmations you read in magazines. So we set about developing a number of simpler, more effective ones that would work for most people.

Like many of the techniques in this book, using affirmation to effect an immediate change in your mood may initially appear too simple and effortless to be effective. But if you use this technique wholeheartedly, without expectation, it will produce the desired result.

The key is to be creative with your wording. For example, if your object is to overcome stress, then you must choose words that are the antithesis of stress – words such as 'calm', 'serene', 'tranquil' and 'relaxed'.

You can add more feeling to it by using thoughts that you can *feel*. For example, 'I radiate this feeling . . . '

Our research shows that people enjoy using the phrase above, not because it's mystical, but because they actually feel a little calmer when they imagine themselves radiating calm or love or positivity. I have no idea why this should be so, it simply works for many people.

Repeat calming words such as these to yourself – as loudly as your environment will allow – until they fill your consciousness. Repeat, repeat, repeat. Do it for at least five minutes. If your mind wanders, just go back to reciting the words as soon as you become aware of it. And, before you know it, they will be taking effect.

All the time in the world

A great many everyday stresses in life relate to time: the belief that there is not enough time to do what you have to do, or the belief that you have too much to do in the time you have available.

The reality is that such stresses have nothing to do with time at all. It's all to do with your perception of it. Clocks do not create time pressure, minds do.

You might think, for example, it would be impossible to find a spare 30 minutes a day to practise Me Time (page 19). But once you've done it a few times, you'll discover that it makes the rest of your day seem much more time-efficient.

Another way to gradually modify your perception of time so that you feel less pressured is the time affirmation.

Consciously, you might think these simple words could not possibly have such a powerful effect. But unconsciously, you'll begin to feel more relaxed from the moment you start using them.

The time affirmation

Whenever you feel that time is getting on top of you, simply repeat the following words to yourself.

'I have all the time in the world.'

Repeat them many times throughout the day. Imagine you can hear them in your own voice. Work them into your inner dialogue so that they become part of your consciousness.

If you wish to embellish, go ahead.

'No matter what is going on in my life, I have all the time in the world.'

While we're on the topic of time, here's a little management technique that makes you feel that you are the master of time rather than the other way around.

The 10-Minute Rule plays on the understanding that you're going to be a bit late on occasions – not because you believe your time is more valuable than someone else's, but because you're a mother and you have an excuse.

The 10-Minute Rule

Most appointments and events in life will succeed just as well whether you're 10 minutes early or 10 minutes late.

- Set out to arrive at all appointments 10 minutes early.
- If you manage to arrive 10 minutes early, you have all that precious time to yourself before making your appointment. Use it to relax and find your balance.
- If you don't arrive early, the *second* 10 minutes come into play. Tell yourself no harm was ever done by someone turning up 10 minutes late for an event.
- Next there's the *third* 10 minutes. Everyone knows that parents of young children have less control over their schedules than other people. Even the most punctual person would grant you an additional 10 minutes because of this fact.

When you add all those lots of 10 minutes together, you suddenly find you always have 30 minutes up your sleeve. What a luxury!

The world's most important job

Many mothers reach a stage when they feel isolated, unappreciated and physically exhausted. Within the framework of round-the-clock duties, a demanding child and sleep deprivation, you may see no end to this stressful spiral.

But there is an end. All you need is a little reassurance along the way. And guess who's the best person to provide that reassurance?

No, it is not your partner. It's you.

The following affirmation is designed to provide the emotional reassurance a mother sometimes needs.

Affirmation of importance

'I have the most important job any person can have. I'm so proud of what I'm achieving.'

Use these words, over and over again, many times a day. Imagine you can hear them in your own voice. Work it in to your inner dialogue so that it becomes part of your consciousness. Hear it over and over again.

If you wish to embellish, go ahead.

'I have the most fulfilling role any human can have. As my baby flourishes, so do I.'

The pregnant affirmation

Pregnancy is a time of wonder and growth. For some women, though, it can also be a time of doubt and insecurity.

What is happening to my body? Will I ever look the same again? Will my baby be fit and well? Will the birth process be traumatic? What will my relationship be like after childbirth? The anxieties at this time can overwhelm some mothers-to-be.

The following affirmation is designed to help you overcome these doubts. Feel free to vary it in any way – as long as it remains positive.

Pregnant affirmation

'As my baby grows, so does my love – for myself, my baby and my partner.'

Use these words, over and over again, many times a day. Imagine you can hear them in your own voice. Work it in to your inner dialogue so that it becomes part of your consciousness. Hear it over and over again.

If you wish to embellish, go ahead.

'I am so proud of my body and the way it gently adapts to create a secure world for my baby.'

The calm parent's affirmation

What if you've been through pregnancy, you feel comfortable and important in your role, but you still feel on edge from time to time?

Following is a general parent's affirmation which will help you feel calm and contented in your role as a parent. Once again, use these words to project the results you want to achieve.

Calm parent affirmation

'I feel enormous love and warmth for my baby. We are happy, calm and peaceful. We radiate this feeling to all we come in contact with.'

Use these words, over and over again, many times a day. Imagine you can hear them in your own voice. Work it in to your inner dialogue so that it becomes part of your consciousness. Hear it over and over again.

If you wish to embellish, go ahead.

'I feel totally confident in my skills and abilities as a mother. I feel at ease with any demands my baby makes. I radiate this confidence to my baby.'

An affirmation of tranquillity

The following affirmation is a general affirmation that communicates a calm, soothing message. Use it like a mantra to impress on your unconscious that you are feeling peaceful and relaxed.

The calm diet

What you eat and drink has a noticeable effect on how you feel. You
know this as soon as you consume any food type. This not only
applies to 'heavy' or 'light' foods, but also to spicy or mild, fatty or
lean, and even restless or calm.

Calm? Could there be such a thing as *calm* food?

There is. You can moderate the way you feel simply by choosing
the appropriate foods and beverages. Some stimulate, while others
help you to relax.

Stimulating foods

These are the foods that cause restlessness and fatigue. At the top of the list are coffee, tea, cola and anything else with caffeine in it.

Closely following this group are foods with chemical additives – artificial preservatives and colourings, artificial flavour enhancers – and processed or refined foods.

Next we come to the spicy foods: those with excessive spices, vinegar, radishes, garlic, onions and the like.

Simply by limiting the amount of such stimulating foods in your diet, you will feel calmer and more relaxed.

Lethargy foods

Another category it's important to consider is lethargy foods. These include meats, alcohol, refined foods and pickled or fermented foods. They have the effect of slowing you down and making you feel sluggish.

Calm foods

Calm foods are the ones to concentrate on. These are easily digested, cleansing, calming and provide maximum energy.

Naturally enough, they include all kinds of fruit, most vegetables, nuts and seeds, beans, grains, dairy products, most herbs and a moderate amount of spices.

When you consume calm foods, you feel lighter and more relaxed.

Carbohydrates play an interesting role. They provide you with energy, and while they can have an elevating effect on your mood, this is often followed by a slump. Proponents of a high-protein, low-carbohydrate diet say that it evens out the emotional ups and downs that sometimes accompany high carbohydrate consumption. Whatever you believe is up to you; your best guide is to gauge the way certain foods affect you.

Guidelines for a calm diet

Experiment with the following, and be guided by the way certain foods affect you:

- Increase the amount of calm foods (fruit, most vegetables, nuts and seeds, beans, grains and milk) in your diet.
- Be moderate with your consumption of lethargy foods (meats, alcohol, refined, pickled or fermented foods).
- Limit or avoid stimulating foods (coffee, tea, cola, spicy foods and those with artificial additives).

Vitamins

Certain vitamins help you resist or recover from the effects of stress. If you structure your diet to highlight the everyday foods that contain these vitamins, chances are you will feel more relaxed as a result. These vitamins include:

- **Vitamin E:** Found in most vegetables, many fruits, eggs and dairy products.

- **Vitamin A:** Found in yoghurt, cream, butter, eggs, liver, carrots, leafy green vegetables and fruit.
- **Vitamin C:** Found in all fruit and vegetables, especially capsicum, blackcurrants, kiwifruit, brussels sprouts, strawberries and oranges.
- **Magnesium:** Found in seeds and wholegrain flour and cereals.
- **Vitamin B:** Found in legumes, lentils, peas, nuts, seeds, wheat germ, bran, wholegrain foods, milk, cheese, yoghurt, meat, fish, poultry and green leafy vegetables.
- **Pantothenic acid (vitamin B5):** Found in peanuts, cabbage, cauliflower, broccoli, liver and eggs.

If you feel you need vitamin supplements, seek the advice of a health-care professional first, particularly if you are pregnant.

Acid–alkaline balance

There are two types of foods in any diet: acid-forming foods and alkaline-forming foods. Acid-forming foods leave an acidic residue after they have been exhausted in your stomach. Alkaline-forming foods leave an alkaline residue.

Acid-forming foods tend to produce unrest. Alkaline-forming foods tend to encourage a restful feeling.

Consume too many acid-producing foods, and you stand a good chance of feeling tense and on edge. Consume a greater proportion of alkaline-forming foods, particularly at stressful times, and you will feel comparatively relaxed and more able to cope.

The converse of this also applies: your moods and emotions influence the acid–alkaline balance in your system. Slow, relaxed breathing encourages alkaline conditions, while tense, shallow breaths generate acid.

By adjusting the balance of these foods in your diet, you can alter the way you feel and become calmer. An ideal ratio is 80 per cent alkaline-forming foods to 20 per cent acid-forming foods.

Alkaline-forming foods	Acid-forming foods
All fresh vegetables	All meat, fish, poultry
All fresh fruits	Eggs and most dairy products
Whole rice and whole flour	Wheat bran, refined flour, seeds
Millet	Sugar, salt, pepper
Molasses	Coffee, tea, cola, alcohol
Dried fruits	Processed and refined foods
Apple cider vinegar	Vinegar (distilled)
Most edible plant matter	Most packaged foods

If you want to choose food that produces a noticeably calm sensation, ensure your diet is high in fresh fruit and vegetables (uncooked as often as possible). In addition, make sure the following foods are well represented on your table: bean sprouts, bananas, kiwifruit, tomatoes, basil, tarragon, legumes, eggs, wheat germ, sesame seeds, milk, yoghurt and oats.

What you drink

The beverages you consume also play a role in how you feel.

For many people, a single cup of coffee is enough to make them feel restless all day – and sometimes into the night as well. Tea, cola and many other fizzy drinks have a similar effect.

These might be attractive options when you're feeling fatigued and in need of a burst of energy. However, like other stimulating foods, they tend to leach your energy after that initial burst, leaving you feeling listless and uneasy as the day wears on. Moreover, after the initial mood enhancement, there is a corresponding downturn which can exacerbate feelings of depression or despondency in some people.

The calm answer is to find alternatives to these stimulating drinks.

If you've been drinking two cups of coffee a day for the past few years, the prospect of replacing this with a herbal tea may seem a little scary. But after you've weaned yourself off the coffee (which may take a few days), you'll notice a distinct elevation in your mood. Some people claim this positive boost can be quite intoxicating.

Water is by far the best alternative to stimulating drinks. It helps you overcome the effects of stress and to remain calm. It also helps in the prevention of hypertension, heart ailments, stroke, respiratory problems, constipation, headache, tooth decay and even the aging process.

The water method

Your intake of water plays a significant role in the way you handle stress.

- Drink at least eight glasses of water each day.
- Drink two glasses on rising, and one before meals.
- Drink water (two sips to one) every time you drink alcohol or coffee.
- Keep a bottle of water wherever you work.
- Drink water from a quality wine glass so it will taste special.
- Drink cool water in preference to fizzy drinks.
- Drink hot water in preference to tea and coffee.

Make a habit of drinking water, and you'll improve your health and increase your ability to stay calm.

Of course, water is not the only alternative to caffeine-laden drinks. Some of the most refreshing beverages are far more exotic.

Peppermint tea is famous for its ability to soothe the nerves and ease digestion. Chamomile tea also works almost immediately as a calming agent. Dandelion 'coffee' doesn't compare with the real thing, but is refreshing and calming. And for a truly calming drink, try milk. Yes, milk.

Milk contains muscle-relaxing properties, plenty of calcium, as well as an amino acid called tryptophan, which helps you relax and feel good.

Tension producer	Calm substitute
coffee	herbal tea dandelion 'coffee' caffeine-free tea green tea water decaffeinated coffee chai milk
tea	peppermint tea chamomile tea rosehip tea fruit teas (without caffeine) hot water with lemon cool water
cola	cold spring water mineral water pure fruit juices

The calm workout

During pregnancy and the first months of motherhood, you may be tempted to abandon nature's most efficient way of burning off excess 'stress chemicals' in your system: exercise.

This would be a great loss. Exercise not only directly counters the effects of negative stress, it also reverses the physical processes that lead to stress. And physical exercise is a powerful weapon against depression, anxiety, worry, and a whole range of emotional and psychological conditions. If you've ever been a regular exerciser, you'll know how good it can make you feel.

Exercise is at its most beneficial – psychologically rather than physically – when it is repetitive and can be performed without thinking. At that point it becomes almost meditative in its effect.

Think about what exercise you might feasibly carry out while pregnant or with your young child. Unless you have a serious medical condition, an ideal calming exercise program for your body involves three to five workouts a week.

Among the many types of 'relaxing' exercise that are suited to pregnant women are yoga, swimming, dancing and Tai Chi. Each of these will help focus your mind positively and gently on your body and your growing baby, as you remain healthy and keep a check on your weight gain. Be aware, however, that while you are pregnant, your resting heart rate and core body temperature are both slightly elevated, so the effect of exercise is more pronounced. For this reason it is wise not to take on more exercise than you are used to, and not to exceed 60–75 per cent of your maximum physical capacity.

If you like the idea of structured programs or exercising as part of a group, consider a gym with a créche so that you can exercise while someone else takes care of your child. Or, if you prefer unstructured exercise, do exactly what comes instinctively when you are stressed – walk.

Walk and be calm

Walking is the perfect exercise for most people. It can even involve your child.

- Walk three to five times a week for 30–45 minutes.
- Walk at a brisk place, but don't worry if you're being overtaken by all the power-walkers.
- If you can't leave your child with someone, take him or her along in a stroller.

Do this regularly and you'll start to feel like a new person – becoming calmer and more stress-free by the day.

The calm home

Although you can see the appeal of having a calm environment in which to raise your children – for your sake as much as your child's – you may wonder whether a calm home and a small child are mutually exclusive.

Even if you could manage it, you'd have to agree that it's hardly in the best interests of a growing child to limit their ability to explore and play – activities that invariably result in a degree of disorder and sometimes even total chaos.

I used to wonder why so many people believed a home clear of clutter was more inclined to be a calm home. When I explored this concept in greater depth, it became evident that an untidy home was an ever-present reminder – to many mothers, in particular – of all the chores they still had to do. This unfinished business was yet another stress in their lives.

While we could argue that parents of young children should be given special dispensation *not* to have to be neat and tidy all the time, that is not the way our psychology works – for many people, physical disarray adds to the tension in their life.

If you feel this way about clutter, you'll be pleased to know there is an easy solution: contain the chaos.

Contain the chaos

If you have the luxury of space, concentrate on keeping certain rooms in shape, while allowing the disarray to exist in others. As soon as you accept this principle, you can exploit it; add to the disarray in the 'untidy room' by dumping your bookwork, ironing and unanswered correspondence in there.

If you don't have the space, create orderly *corners* of the house. Concentrate on keeping these spic and span, while you leave other areas to the forces of nature.

Noise

Although noise and children go hand in hand, noise tends to raise the tension levels of a household.

This is not always immediately obvious. If you spend a lot of time alone with your child, you may welcome a little noisy distraction from time to time. Some derive a degree of human comfort from leaving the radio or television on in the background. But however benign this sound may appear, it does extract a toll. And for most people, constant noise induces a degree of restlessness.

So enjoy all the noise you want, but intersperse it with periods of quiet. At certain times throughout the day, make an effort to listen for the silence and try to carry some of that feeling around with you. Silence is the essence of calm. Revel in it.

The Calm Space

Calm Space is one of the most powerful calming mechanisms you can create in your home. Its purpose is to provide a refuge you can escape to in moments of tension or pressure. And its beauty is that it is equally as pleasing for you as it is for your child, your partner and your dog.

To be effective, you must 'train' this place to produce the calm you desire (or, more correctly, train yourself to associate feeling calm with a specific place). It doesn't matter where this Calm Space is in your home – it might be a seat in the garden or in the corner of your bedroom – the important thing is the way you feel about it.

After a while, you will be able to use this as a place to retreat to whenever you feel tense or under pressure. All you have to do is turn up and allow your previous calm associations to come flooding back.

The Calm Space

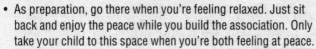

- Nominate an area in your home to 'train' as your Calm Space.
- As preparation, go there when you're feeling relaxed. Just sit back and enjoy the peace while you build the association. Only take your child to this space when you're both feeling at peace.
- Add a ritual – remove your shoes, use a soft voice, play calming music, burn oils.
- Go to your Calm Space whenever you want to feel more relaxed.

Calm music

You know from experience that music can have a powerful effect on your mood and emotions. But it can do more than that: it can induce real physiological changes – altering your heartbeat, breathing rhythm, blood pressure, hormone levels, brainwave activity and even your immune response.

In a home environment, music can be a powerful way of spreading calm – if you choose the right music.

The starting point is to look for music that suits your taste. If your taste is for the classics, romantics, modern orchestral or jazz, there is a wealth of material to explore. Relaxing chants and gospel and choral music are also widely available.

You'll have to search a little harder if you prefer popular artists, but some of the slower, more moody albums will work. The challenge is finding albums that maintain the mood from beginning to end.

Then there's the category that record stores label anything from 'World Music', 'New Age' to 'Mind Body Spirit'. This includes material ranging from ambient sounds to the musically complex. You will invariably find something soothing and to your taste in this section if you persist. (For more information on calm music, visit www.calmcentre.com/sounds)

Soothing with calm music

Search within the musical categories you feel most at home with. Choose with your heart rather than your head.

What *feels* right? What soothes?

Use different types of music for different types of mood, especially with your baby:

- relaxed music for playtime
- even slower music for quiet time
- very slow, uncomplicated music for bedtime

The most popular way to use calm music is to allow it to weave its effect in the background of your normal activities. However, music can play an even more calming role when you concentrate on it. Have you ever listened to a piece and been 'transported' by it? This can be a profoundly calming experience.

Several years ago my research group, The Calm Centre, commissioned an album called 'Deep Calm' to create just this effect. With 'Deep Calm', concentrating on any one sound at the beginning of the piece leads you to become calmer as the journey continues.

While this worked particularly well for mothers, adults of all types, troubled adolescents and some babies, it had varying effects on young children. Whether this was a matter of taste, psychology or musical development, we couldn't determine.

So what does work best for young ones?

In the 1950s, researcher Dr Salk discovered that the sound of an adult human heartbeat helped calm a child and organise the immature central nervous system. Considering that a baby lives with an adult heartbeat sound for the first nine months, this is no surprise. So heartbeat 'music' became all the rage.

In the 1960s, we learnt that when women sang or played certain calming music during pregnancy, their newborns were calmed by – and showed a preference for – the same compositions. The womb's amniotic fluid is an excellent conductor of sound, so playing calming music during pregnancy may be a powerful way of communicating and bonding with your unborn baby.

Then researchers discovered what you probably already knew all along: babies are calmed and physically attracted to harmonious melodies, and agitated by discord and wide variances in dynamic range. Lullabies are a good example of effective calming tunes.

Whatever your preference, music can be a delightful way to create a calm, nurturing environment for both you and your baby.

Deep Relaxation

Deep relaxation. Just the thought of it will make you feel more restful. However, the benefits of deep states of calm go much further than this. Being able to access them on an ongoing basis has long-term benefits. For example, you will be:

- less affected by sleep deprivation
- more able to cope and deal with stress
- more positive and tolerant
- more adept at juggling various relationships
- happier and more contented

Not only is this possible, a number of the simple methods that follow will show you how easily it can be achieved.

Steps to Deep Relaxation

Whatever is going on around you right now, just pause for a second – right now – and turn your attention to your breathing.

- Be aware of how it sounds.
- Be aware of how each breath goes, slowly and deeply, to a restful place within you.
- Be aware only of this breath.
- Be aware of how relaxed it helps you to feel.

One minute of this and you will be calmer and more relaxed. Twenty minutes of it and you will ease into a state of Deep Relaxation. Your thoughts will begin to still, and your mind, body and spirit will begin to enjoy a blissful period of absolute harmony. There is nothing you can do to prevent it; it will happen of its own accord.

Breathing Calm

The human body has a number of involuntary functions – pulse, heartbeat, breathing and so on. These take place whether you're conscious or unconscious. Of all these involuntary functions, only breathing is subject to any level of conscious control.

By controlling the way you breathe, you can influence the way you feel. You can also influence the way you think, your mood, even your health and wellbeing. This is why breathing techniques are so commonly used to encourage calm, to help the body to heal, to help overcome adversity and to help you perform – physically as well as mentally – in ways you might not normally be able to.

And, even more beautiful, Breathing Calm is easily achieved in three simple steps.

Breathe deeply

One of the most visible characteristics of a person under stress is the way they breathe: each breath comes quickly and is quite shallow.

A relaxed person, on the other hand, breathes more deeply and slowly.

If you modify your rate of breathing so that it emulates a relaxed person (that is, each breath is slow and deep), you will start to relax.

So let's start with a deep breath. Try it yourself, now.

If you tried, chances are you pulled in your chin, puffed out your chest, and lifted your shoulders as you filled your lungs. This is how you were taught to do it in kindergarten.

But the way to take a really deep breath, to really fill your lungs with air, does not involve these actions at all. It means concentrating on the *bottom* of your lungs, sucking the air in right down *low*.

If you want to see a demonstration of this, watch your sleeping baby. With each breath, you'll see the stomach rise and fall, not the chest.

You can practise this yourself, it just requires the use of your imagination.

Instead of imagining the air going in through your mouth and down into your lungs, imagine it coming in at the base of your lungs (down low near your navel) and flowing upwards.

In this way you will feel your lower abdomen e-x-p-a-n-d as the air sucks in.

Breathing deeply this way makes a huge difference to the way you feel.

Breathe slowly

The next step is easier: consciously slow down your rate of breathing. Just a little. No need for any great exertion – just be aware of it slowing slightly.

Listen

The third step is to listen. Concentrate on the sound of your breath as it comes and goes. Listen to the inflow of air through your nostrils. Listen to the sound of your warm breath as you breathe out through your mouth.

That's all you have to do: **breathe deeply, breathe slowly** and **listen.** You will notice a calming effect after a couple of minutes – and the more often you do it, the faster it takes effect.

Breathing Calm

- Breathe deeply – right down low into your lungs.
- Breathe slowly – just a little.
- Listen to your breath as it comes and goes.

Deep Calm

My first book on the topic of calm was *The Calm Technique.* It centres around a specific technique that is really a traditional meditation method stripped of its mystical connotations. What follows is a variation of this, known as Deep Calm.

A common response to the topic of meditation is: 'Oh, I must learn how to meditate . . . one day.' This is based on the belief that meditation is a skill, like yoga, which has to be worked on and perfected before it is of any use. Not so.

While it can be practised, and will become more effective the more often you use it, meditation is not a skill that requires any great learning or discipline. Indeed, with a minimum of effort and instruction, anyone can use Deep Calm; *everyone* can reap the benefits from it.

As you can imagine, Deep Calm brings a multitude of benefits to mothers who are required to deal with the day-to-day stresses of looking after a baby. You may have heard of meditation defined as 'being, not doing'. For mothers who are 'doing' all day long, the chance to sit quietly and 'be' may seem like an unaffordable luxury. Yet, if you can set aside just 15–30 minutes at the beginning or end of each day, you will find the inevitable process of 'doing' in your life so much easier to accommodate.

Those who use Deep Calm say it's the one state in which they feel totally natural and at peace. During Deep Calm you will be relaxed in both mind and body: your breathing and heart rate slow; your thoughts are clear; you may even feel like you're floating. You have a sense of serenity and detachment which may be accompanied by strong feelings of certainty and security.

Deep Calm seeks to replicate those deeply relaxed feelings you might already associate with other experiences. Think of how you feel when you are:

- daydreaming
- in the twilight world just before you fall asleep
- having a massage
- on a long train ride, staring out the window

At times like these you aren't particularly aware of any specific state of mind, you are just being. This is the aim of Deep Calm.

Deep Calm preparation

The preparation stage of Deep Calm can be a delightfully calming routine in its own right.

First of all, find yourself a place where you can sit and relax, without interruption, for 15–30 minutes. Take the phone off the hook.

The next steps are all done with the eyes.

You know from your own experience that one of the fastest and most predictable ways to ease into a state of relaxation is simply to close your eyes. This one simple action has an immediate calming effect on the entire body.

But first, there is a step called decon- 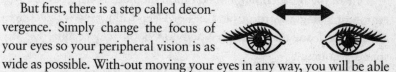 vergence. Simply change the focus of your eyes so your peripheral vision is as wide as possible. With-out moving your eyes in any way, you will be able to take in more of the room around you.

How much you can see is not important; it's the *feeling* we're trying to create. Your eye muscles begin to relax as your peripheral vision widens.

Next, lower your lids. With your  eyes still deconverged, slowly lower your eyelids (a). You will notice how your body begins to relax. This happens of its own accord.

Finally, allow your eyes to drift upwards (b), just a little.

When you are in a meditative state, your eyes drift up involuntarily. You probably notice this happening in the moments before you fall asleep. Consciously reproducing this action creates a similarly restful effect.

Widen your peripheral vision, lower your lids, then let your eyes drift upwards. Following these three steps over about a minute will automatically help you to relax.

The Deep Calm method

You achieve Deep Calm when you stop thinking, or still your thoughts. The only way to consciously do this is to fill your mind with just one thing – an image, a fantasy, a feeling, a repetitive action, or a word or a phrase – so there is no room for anything else.

One of the most common meditation methods consists of the repetition of a single word or phrase. For Deep Calm, any word chosen at random from the dictionary or phonebook will be fine. Or any sound you fancy.

The one I like is 'calm'. Or you could try 'calming'.

All that matters about this word is its repetition. Speak it aloud for a minute or so, until you're used to hearing the word spoken in your own voice, then imagine it from there on. Over and over again.

That's all there is to it. In your mind, hear yourself saying this word over and over again. When your attention strays, and it will, simply direct it back to the word. Calmly redirect your attention back to that word.

Deep Calm

- Sit somewhere quiet where you won't be disturbed, preferably on a comfortable, straight-backed chair.
- Perform the three steps of preparation (widen your peripheral vision, close your eyes, let them drift upwards).
- Listen to the sound of your breathing.
- When you feel relaxed, hear the word you have chosen coming from somewhere inside your head – as if you were speaking it yourself.
- As you breathe in, listen for the word; as you breathe out, hear the word.
- When your attention wanders, calmly redirect it to the word. Continue for 15–30 minutes.

Remember, the effect of Deep Calm is slow, subtle and cumulative. Similar to an exercise program, it works best when performed regularly for a reasonable length of time. And, just like an exercise program, your initial enthusiasm may wane after a month or so, but this is precisely when you may start to notice its ongoing benefits. If you continue for a couple of months, you are unlikely to want to stop.

Love and touch

Building on our research into Deep Calm, we discovered that it's possible to create deeply relaxed states simply by the thoughts you have.

Foremost among these are thoughts that relate to love, or to deep spiritual conviction (such as thinking about God in one of His/Her many forms).

Similarly, those who have deep and loving thoughts about someone else – such as a child or partner – will find themselves easing into a relaxed state. If you continue thinking these thoughts without interruption, you'll find yourself entering into an even more relaxed state, not unlike Deep Calm.

The human touch can also have this effect – if you use the Deep Calm technique while you're nursing or holding a resting child, for example, you can slip into the most profound state of relaxation.

A gentle touch from another person works wonders in relaxing you. This can be achieved through intimacy with someone close to you, as well as through massage or reflexology, both of which have the ability to take you straight through to Deep Calm without any effort on your part.

chapter three

Calm for your child

One joy dispels a hundred cares.

Confucius

Your child's development

Although the focus of this book is helping *you* enjoy a calm frame of mind, your child's frame of mind is closely related. When your child is calm, you'll find it easier to be calm.

However, a child's needs and motivations will generally be less consistent than your own, tending to vary from one stage of development to the next.

The following sections relate to each stage of that development: from pregnancy through to preschool age.

Refer to the relevant section when the time comes. Not only will this make it easier for you to understand what your child is experiencing, it will also address the challenges you may to need to manage for yourself during this phase.

At all times, though, remember that your child is unique – all children grow and develop in their own special way, seldom conforming to what others believe is the 'norm'.

Pregnancy

For some women, pregnancy is a time of serenity and wonder – when you float about feeling healthy, vital and emotionally fulfilled. Others see it as a time of tiredness, physical discomfort and emotional swings. Somewhere in between is the experience of most.

It's often said that extreme stress or worry may exacerbate problems with pregnancy, labour and breastfeeding, and may even play a role in morning sickness and postnatal depression.

Perhaps this is true. However, one thing we can be sure of is that remaining calm is better for you and your baby than feeling stressed – if for no other reason than it will make you feel better *now*.

There are sound reasons to approach motherhood relaxed and rested. For a start, the mother who nurtures herself will be better able to nurture her baby. And, while labour itself is an exhausting process, it is only the beginning. The months after the baby's arrival demand almost complete devotion from the mother, possibly involving disrupted sleep and round-the-clock duties. Being fit, calm and rested helps you cope with this marathon.

Pregnancy can be a time of consolidation and preparation, a time to concentrate on relaxation, exercise and diet – topics covered earlier in this book. But it is also a time to establish a general calming routine that will serve you, not only today, but in all the months and years following the birth of your child.

Start to develop a program of calm thoughts and exercises now. Then this will be one less thing to have to think about once baby arrives.

Childbirth

Before we examine the various ways of introducing calm into the process of childbirth, let's examine why childbirth induces trepidation in some parents-to-be.

At the top of the list is fear. Fear of pain. Fear of hospitals. Fear of complications, loss of dignity and control. Fear of the unknown. Some of these fears become self-fulfilling. Fear of pain, for example, leads to tension, which tends to amplify pain.

Yet most fears stem from ignorance or inexperience – both of which can be overcome with knowledge and familiarity.

Knowledge comes from books and from talking with women who've borne children themselves.

Familiarity comes from experience and rehearsal. This is what antenatal courses are for. Typically, these courses consist of several sessions involving fathers as well as mothers, and incorporate lectures, videos, practice sessions and a visit to the delivery rooms. It is remarkable how much more confident you feel after attending these.

But knowing how to relax and remain calm in physically stressful situations such as childbirth requires forethought and practice. Antenatal courses will teach you some of these methods. In addition, you can employ any of the suggestions from this book. *But please practise them well in advance of the day*. Then you will have a base level of calm you can depend on, regardless of what delivery-room techniques you supplement them with.

The important thing to bear in mind is that all kinds of calming techniques are useful – and the ones that will work best for you are the ones you *feel* will work best for you at any given time. Experiment with a few, and practise until you can use them without a second thought.

The first 6 months

Welcome to parenthood!

You're in at the deep end: all those months of preparation and training, but no time to reflect on what has taken place. The first few days of motherhood are, for many women, a surreal time, with most of the responsibilities being taken care of by someone more experienced or qualified than you.

Then you arrive home with your new bundle. If you're like most new parents, you feel completely unprepared for what lies ahead. And, from the moment your baby lets out its first big cry, the pressure is on.

Your days and nights begin to blur. Sleep becomes a fantasy. Your beauty regime is put on hold.

Then, just when you think your whole life is going to continue this way, a miraculous change takes place. Your baby starts sleeping at the same time each day and for the same length of time. More pleasing still, your child recognises you – and smiles! Nothing can prepare you for the feelings of love and attachment that follow. That's what makes it all worthwhile.

The world of your newborn

Age	Physical development	Mental development	Understanding	Behaviour
0–3 months	Near-sighted; can just make out light, shapes and movement Eyes track close movements Hearing well developed, smell slightly less so	Brain stem well developed to control life's basic functions (breathing etc)	Has empathy for your emotions	Smiles faintly Reflex in search of feed Turns toward sounds Aware of hands and feet Cries often Likes being held
4–6 months	Transfixed by moving objects, especially anything brightly coloured and close Eyesight is quite sharp Developing own immune system (minor infections are possible) Can grasp objects	Brain can respond to all sounds involved in language	Listens intently and recognises own name when spoken Prefers mother to most others	Smiles often Laughs Watches you intently Imitates certain sounds Explores objects with mouth Tries to sit up

Until recently, it was thought that a child perceived very little in the first few months of life. A newborn was like a blank slate onto which a personality, routines and habits were written. Research over recent decades, however, has given us greater insight into this world.

Now we know babies possess innate social instincts that begin to flower in the very first dealings with their mother. By their eighth day of life, a newborn can distinguish the smell of their mother. Soon the newborn loves to hear the sound of human voices, especially that of their mother. The baby prefers to look at visual patterns that replicate the human face and, once again, prefers her face to others.

While the newborn does not comprehend in adult terms, they are acutely aware of their environment, which they experience through physical sensations. These extend to the mother, whom they experience as an extension of themself.

The most obvious strains that characterise this period relate to **crying**, **dependency** and **environment**.

Crying

Most babies spend up to 7 per cent of their day crying. What does this mean? Is it illness? Is it distress or irritation? Wind? A baby's way of making 'conversation'?

Crying is one of the few communication methods your baby has. While it's usually an indication of discomfort of some kind, crying is never an attempt at being vexatious or manipulative – a baby of this age simply does not understand how to use their behaviour to influence the actions of another person. So there is no merit in the belief that picking up a baby when they cry only encourages this behaviour.

It's more calming for both you and your newborn if you 'give in' and comfort them.

Dependency

From the first moments of life after childbirth, you and your baby are a unit. Your baby needs you to regulate every aspect of their life. For this reason, your baby is instinctively attuned to you and even your most subtle responses. If you hold them stiffly, they will squirm. If you react with alarm, so will your baby. If you leave baby crying, they will feel incomplete and alone. Newborns require gentle, soothing contact as much as possible.

At around three months, you'll have noticed just how much of an individual your child has become. Your baby is able to interact effectively through smiles and cooing sounds, no longer through crying alone.

By now your child craves social interaction and may cry from loneliness if left alone for too long. At the same time they become fussier about who is with them and who picks them up. Your baby is learning to discriminate.

Environment

It may seem obvious, but a newborn thrives in a calm environment.

For nine months, your baby existed in a tranquil, carefree world where every need was met without them even knowing. Now your child is beginning to experience monumental change: they feel hunger and need to learn how to feed; they need to learn how to sleep and be awake; they are learning about light, sound, cold, warmth and texture. But above all, your baby needs rest – between 14 and 15.5 hours per day.

Handling your newborn

A newborn is a little bundle of instincts. Your instinct will probably be to hold and protect your baby. To ensure that these interactions are as calm and nurturing as possible, there are a number of things to keep in mind.

The calm way to handle a newborn

- Hold your baby gently, calmly and firmly, preferably with the tummy against your body. As the neck muscles are not yet developed, ensure that you support the head. Rough play will make your child feel insecure.
- Speak in a soft, reassuring voice.
- Maintain eye contact at all times.
- Avoid bright lights and startling noises.
- Bathe your baby in tepid water – warm but not hot. And, when changing, try to do so gently and in stages.
- Most important of all, try to be as relaxed as possible whenever you handle your newborn.

While the demands of your baby can be time-consuming and tiring, these first months lay the foundation for future development. Your child needs you to understand their needs and idiosyncrasies, to establish their boundaries and routines, and to remain calm throughout the process.

There are a number of considerations that will impact on this.

These range from **your baby's temperament,** to **sleep and settling techniques,** to the way you deal with **crying**.

Your baby's temperament

Despite what some experts would have you believe, babies seldom conform to a particular norm. From the moment they arrive in this world, they begin to develop and exert their own personalities.

Many believe that personality traits shown at this stage have a strong bearing on the type of care a child receives, and may even influence the opportunities they attract as they grow up. For example, a calm, easy-going baby often makes it easier for you to respond in a warm and loving way – a reaction that encourages growth and continues throughout the child's life. On the other hand, a more 'difficult' baby may make it harder for you to maintain a calm and accommodating attitude. Please remember, though, just as all babies are different, so too are all parents.

Over the first few months, you and your baby not only have to negotiate the ordinary day-to-day interactions of carer and child, but you also need to accommodate each other's personalities. And, you guessed it, this requires more accommodation from you than from your baby.

It helps, therefore, to understand the temperament of your baby, and how it can best be accommodated. Consider the following:

- What is your child's activity level? Does your baby try to find their way to the other end of the room when you put them on the floor? Or is your child less animated, content to remain where they're placed?

- Are the biological rhythms (sleeping, feeding, bodily functions) of your child reasonably regular, or are they unpredictable?
- How does your baby react to new things? Are new toys, experiences and faces received well?
- How intensely does your child respond to stimuli?
- Is your child's mood primarily calm, or strained and agitated?
- Can you easily distract your child from crying or contrary behaviour?

Answering these questions will give you the first indications of your child's temperament.

When reading through the 'types' below, keep in mind that these are based on stereotypes. Your child is unique, and cannot be pigeon-holed with any accuracy.

In addition, your own temperament will colour the way you perceive your baby's temperament. If, for example, you prefer a strict routine and you are fastidious about the administration of your home, a wakeful baby may seem problematic to you. Conversely, if you're more relaxed in your attitude and don't mind if domestic organisation goes by the wayside for a time, a wakeful baby might be a positive thing.

So please treat what follows as an indication only.

Furthermore, since this is a book about calm, with the underlying suggestion that a calm parent often has a calm child, there may be a risk you will apply this measure to your own circumstances – maybe even feeling a little guilty if your baby does not appear calm.

Once again, it's important to remember that all humans are different – even babies. Some babies respond to a calm parent, others don't.

Some need a special approach and special care, others do not. Some require an extra degree of firm handling, while others do not.

So let's look at some of the more common temperament types.

The cry-baby

For some mothers, this baby can be a handful. Cry-babies do everything (except, of course, crying) by halves. They don't feed very well and they don't sleep very well. They don't like too much stimulation, but grizzle when there's not enough. They often seem miserable but don't comfort easily.

It can be difficult caring for a child going through this stage, if indeed it is a stage. Your soothing efforts usually go unrewarded and often achieve nothing but more crying. Having to deal with this at 3 a.m., after months of broken sleep, takes some of the gloss off being a parent.

Whatever the reason for it, the 'cry-baby' phase is usually temporary and can often be eased with a few simple strategies.

Strategies for the cry-baby

- Ensure your baby is getting sufficient milk.
- Ensure they are warm enough or cool enough.
- Carry your baby in a sling or papoose so they can remain close to you as much as possible.

The sensitive baby

The sensitive baby wakes at the slightest sound or movement. This type of baby resents having their clothes changed or being bathed, and shrieks when someone holds them awkwardly. Just watch out if the telephone rings, someone switches on a light, or a car alarm goes off in the street!

The sensitive baby needs calm and gentle handling. Generally, they grow out of this oversensitivity as they mature.

Strategies for the sensitive baby

- Take care not to startle with sudden movement, light or sound.
- Bathe your baby as infrequently as practical; 'top and tail' them at other times.
- When changing their clothes, try to do it in stages so that your baby is never fully exposed.
- When introducing new toys or people, observe your child's responses carefully.

The wakeful baby

As any parent quickly discovers, you can't force a baby to sleep. But some babies are less cooperative than others in this area.

Wakeful babies who are happy while they're awake are usually just not ready to go to sleep, and expect to be entertained in the meantime. While at times this can be entertaining for you, too, you may struggle to see the entertainment value when it happens in the middle of the night.

Wakeful babies who are miserable while they're awake are another matter. In this case you need to consider other indicators such as feeding and overtiredness.

When it comes to wakeful babies, you have two choices: change the baby's habits or change your own. Since it's next to impossible to change your child's habits, it's advisable to opt for changing your own. This need not be as big a compromise at it seems. It is a matter of integrating your wakeful baby into the general routine of your life.

Strategies for the wakeful baby

- Go with the flow. Accept that all babies are different and, at this moment, your baby is simply exercising their individuality.
- Make sure your child isn't in need of food or sleep.
- Make your baby part of the normal routines of your day. Cleaning, shopping, typing and gardening can all be done with baby in a sling or resting nearby.
- Look after your own rest needs. Sleep when your baby sleeps.

The sleepy baby

Believe it or not, there are babies who sleep more than is good for them. It isn't that they get too much sleep, it's that their sleep habits can interfere with other aspects of their development.

The sleepy baby may not spend enough time interacting with the environment around them. Sometimes a sleepy baby might find it difficult to gain weight since they miss out on feeding as often as they should. If so, it's important to compensate for these activities while your baby is awake.

But if your child is feeding well, and is stimulated when awake, relax and enjoy the extra time you get for yourself – it's something some mothers would give their eye teeth for.

Strategies for the sleepy baby

- Ensure your child receives more than usual stimulation while they're awake.
- If sleep interferes with your baby's eating, it may be necessary to wake them for feeds. Don't rely too much on demand feeding.
- Enjoy the extra time, and don't tell other mothers!

Sleep and settling techniques

How do you get your baby to sleep whenever, and for as long as, you'd like them to? For most mothers, this is the topic nearest and dearest to your pillow.

If they're not worked on early, sleep issues can remain a major bugbear throughout childhood. Not only does this lead to ongoing disruption for you, but it is hardly conducive to a calm environment for the rest of the family.

Most newborns do not sleep through the night. They need to be fed every four hours or so, sometimes less. If you're breastfeeding, this will probably mean you'll be on call round the clock – not altogether an attractive proposition after the rigours of childbirth. A supportive partner helps, but even if they take over many of these nightly duties, chances are you'll still be affected by broken sleep.

Sleep cycles of a newborn

While babies do not generally conform to any sleep cycle standard, a fairly common pattern is:

0–6 weeks: Baby will eat and sleep with very little activity in between. If you notice that your newborn becomes restless at a certain time of the day, take note and adjust your daily activities accordingly.

6–12 weeks: Baby will probably begin to stay awake for an hour or so after a feed, followed by a sleep for 2–3 hours.

4 months: Your baby will now stay awake longer and sleep for shorter periods (perhaps 2 hours at a time). At this stage your baby is aware of their environment and likes things to remain the same in their sleeping area. If you have not instituted a sleeping ritual by now, it may be time to do so – you'll reap the benefits later when your baby has learnt to keep awake deliberately.

6 months: Your child now requires just two sleeps during the day – one in the morning and one in the afternoon. Your baby is, or soon will be, capable of sleeping 8–10 hours at a stretch.

Where is the best place for a newborn to sleep?

There may be good reasons for having your baby sleep in the same room as you, but there are disadvantages. For a start, you'll probably spend more time awake than you need to. You may also be over-solicitous to your child's noises and cries and, in checking, may disturb their rest.

At around four to five months, it may be advisable to allow your baby to sleep elsewhere, as they are now more aware of things around them and can easily be woken by *your* noises during the night. If you feel uneasy about this move, an electronic baby monitor will allow you to sleep in another room while still hearing your child's every move and cry.

Settling

Ideally, your baby will learn how to settle themselves without your intervention. The sooner your baby does this, the more harmonious life becomes for all.

A baby who is confident of their boundaries and that their needs will be met, will usually take less time to settle than a baby who lacks that sense of security. Anything you can do to reassure your child of their place in your world should pay dividends. If you heed their cries and attend to their needs with tenderness, your baby is likely to become more compliant as time goes on.

Probably the most important settling skill you can learn at this stage is how to identify signs of tiredness. In the early months, most settling problems will be overcome simply by putting baby down at the right time. If you determine this moment well, sleep comes easily. There are three tell-tale signs when your baby is ready for sleep:

- Your baby will begin to make jerky, uncoordinated movements, and possibly ball up their hands.
- They will start to grimace and frown.
- They will grizzle with increasing intensity.

Beware of the grizzle! You may be able to stop it temporarily by picking up or distracting your baby, but chances are they will start again and the restless behaviour will become more pronounced. Your child will then be a bundle of tense, grumpy energy and will not only require more effort in settling, but will probably wake after 10 or 20 minutes and need settling all over again.

First-step settling techniques

Bearing in mind that your baby cannot keep awake deliberately before about eight months, here are a few methods you can use to settle them:

Establish a sleep ritual: When you put your baby to bed, do the same things in the same order every time. This will help your child realise that it is now sleep time.

Make your baby feel secure: Wrapping or swaddling has a soothing effect on most babies; it invokes feelings of being in the womb (we assume) and secures the hands so baby doesn't fling them about and wake up. However, some babies prefer 'hands-free', so play it by ear. ▶

Pat your baby: With your baby's body pressed against yours, pat them firmly and rhythmically on the bottom, or rub their back. Enhance this by singing or shushing gently into your baby's ear.

Rock your baby: Rocking simulates the movement of the baby in the womb while walking. You can reproduce this effect with a cradle, a bassinet on wheels, or a pram. Sometimes it helps to do this quite vigorously, although always in a controlled, regular motion. Around 60 rocks per minute seems to work well.

Some say a baby should be discouraged from falling asleep at the breast or bottle as they will learn to depend on a sated feeling to settle themselves. If your child falls asleep this way, you may find them wide awake shortly after putting them bed. Better to put your child to bed well after the feed.

Temperature control

You know from your own experience that too much or too little warmth can have a detrimental effect on the quality of your sleep. This also applies to your baby. While babies can regulate their own body temperature to an extent, they obviously cannot add or remove clothing and bedcovers to find the most comfortable arrangement. They need you to do this for them.

But how do you determine what is a comfortable temperature, and if they need more or less covering?

In cold conditions this is not so difficult, but warmth presents other problems. Even if their hands and feet are cool to the touch, your baby may still be too warm. A more reliable indicator is feeling the back of the neck or under the arms for temperature and to check if there's any perspiration.

Take extra care if you carry your baby in a sling, because *your* body warmth needs to be taken into account as well. Your baby will then probably need less cladding.

Out-of-cradle settling techniques

If first-step settling techniques prove ineffective, here are three out-of-cradle settling techniques that require a little more effort on your part, but are still effective.

Baby-buggying: This is the first recourse of many parents when baby has squalled themself purple and no amount of settling has taken effect. A long stroll with the pram can work wonders. A variation of this is the 'pram rock': finding a nice little bump in the pavement and rocking the pram backwards and forwards over it.

Baby-driving: This used to be our family's settling technique of last resort. Take your baby for a spin around town in the car. The driving motion often lulls them to sleep after a while. If this doesn't work, turn on the music; even if the lullaby or symphony doesn't bring on sleep, it will help drown out the crying. Of course, this technique presents a small problem after you've got your baby to sleep – how do you get a baby out of the car seat and back into bed without waking them? (I've slept in the car before.)

Baby-slinging: There is a variety of baby slings on the market that allow you to carry your baby, without using your hands, while you walk or work. ▶

You can make dinner, walk to the shops, take yourself off for coffee, or simply pace up and down the hallway, with baby there all the way. The combination of walking and being close to an adult heartbeat is a potent sleep inducer, and most babies will settle this way. A sling offers a dual benefit: you can take yourself for a brisk, stimulating walk while baby is snoozing.

The dummy

Opinions polarise on the humble dummy: some mothers swear by them; others think they're ghastly. You and your infant are the most qualified to judge.

There is no question that it offers welcome relief for some babies, though a breastfed baby may not take to it so readily. However, there are some caveats:

- If you are breastfeeding, a dummy can interfere with your baby's sucking technique. It may be advisable to wait until your baby is able to attach well to the nipple.
- Some babies become dependent on their dummy to fall asleep. Then, if they lose it during the night, they will protest until everyone in the house is awake.
- Overdependence on a dummy can mean your baby doesn't learn to entertain or comfort themselves by any means other than having something in their mouth.
- Badly designed dummies may cause orthodontic problems later in childhood. Make sure you choose one that is designed with your child's developing needs in mind.

Bathing

Most babies are soothed by the feeling of warm water on their skin. This is why bathtime and bedtime go so well together. To strengthen this association, you can make bathing part of the bedtime ritual. It can become a relaxing event for both of you.

First, prepare the bath. A small baby bath is easier to use, and it makes your child feel safer and more comfortable.

Water temperature should be tepid – test it on the sensitive skin on the inside of your arm. Place a sponge in the bath and a warm towel nearby.

To ensure the bathing experience is calming, relax your child as much as possible *before* you place them in the water. Trying to bathe a squirming, protesting infant can be counterproductive.

Hold your baby with your wrist or arm supporting the head and your hand grasping the upper arm from beneath. In this way, your baby can look up at you for reassurance, kicking their legs quite vigorously if they wish, without sliding around too much.

When the bath is completed, wrap them as swiftly and snugly as possible in a towel.

Massage

Baby massage is another calming technique to add to your daily ritual. Studies show that babies who receive regular massage gain weight faster and sleep more soundly than those who do not. Certainly massage helps dispense with the stress hormones that affect all humans – even young ones.

While baby massage may not always be a settling technique in its own right, it usually engenders a loving sense of calm and tenderness for both you and your baby. Its object is to coax your child into a restful frame of mind – during their awake time – not to force them to sleep.

The technique required is both basic and intuitive.

Baby massage

- To begin with, make the room comfortable and warm. Lower the lights and maybe play some relaxing music.

- Warm your hands.

- Warm a little baby oil to just above room temperature.

- Spread some oil over the area to be massaged.

- Begin by resting the palms of your hands on your baby's body until you can feel their body heat. Wait another 30 seconds.

- Now, using your fingertips, gently massage in light, even strokes.

- Take your feedback from your baby. If baby becomes tense or cries, vary your movement. For small babies, it sometimes helps to hold the legs up to the tummy so that they are curled comfortably.

- Concentrate on baby's legs, hips, feet, bottom and back. Some babies enjoy massage on their tummies. If your baby likes it, try stroking the neck and shoulders.

- When you've finished and your baby is relaxed, stay with them for a few minutes and share in the warmth and mellowness.

Naturally, not all settling techniques work for all babies. It's important to respect your child's individuality. Experiment with different techniques, but be patient, taking care not to keep switching from one to the next. For example, if you choose rocking or patting, allow a good five minutes for it to begin to take effect.

Sometimes settling takes extra effort. And you'll soon appreciate that your baby's time expectations are never as compelling as your own.

Whatever action you take, the most important ingredient in calming your baby is your own frame of mind. Children are adept at picking up on tensions or distractions.

Your child will be much more receptive to your attempts to calm, when you're calm and ordered within yourself – or, more importantly, when your *approach* is calm. By adopting a calm approach, or the Calm Role (page 35), it's possible to convince anyone, even yourself, that you're calm.

Crying

The accepted wisdom is that an average newborn will cry for around 2 hours in every 24. So, even allowing for the fact that your baby is an individual and may or may not conform to this norm, you can probably expect a fair amount of noise in the average day.

Crying is your baby's form of communication. It may be instinctive, but it is still an attempt at communication and often indicates that your baby is either uncomfortable in some way or has a need that is not being satisfied. Sometimes it is just your baby's way of relieving tension. As your child matures, you may hear them experimenting when they're alone, trying different sounds and inflections.

Why does my baby cry?

If you haven't already done so, you'll soon learn to distinguish the various types of cries. Often they will occur because of one of the following reasons:

- hunger
- wind
- cold or overheating
- soiled nappy
- overstimulation, such as keeping your baby up when tired
- understimulation, such as when they are bored or ignored
- physical pain
- being startled with light or sound, or being undressed
- poor timing, such as waiting too long for a feed, feeding at the wrong rate, putting them to bed at the wrong time
- loneliness or lack of contact

If you suspect your baby's cries are an indication of ill health, seek assistance from a health-care professional.

In the first six weeks, though, babies cry even when nothing appears to be wrong.

Calming a crying baby

- Begin by trying to identify the cause of the crying. Mentally go through the checklist of possible reasons, then choose the appropriate action. Don't leave your baby crying for too long, as this can exacerbate matters.

- Pick up and cuddle your baby. Human contact, especially when it is skin against skin, has an immediate calming effect.

- Feed your baby. (See feeding issues on pages 95–96.)

- Maintain eye contact. Make sure your baby can see you are calm and happy.

- Watch for signs of tiredness, and put to bed if baby is sleepy.

- Change your baby's nappy or clothes. Sometimes these can become irritating, and a simple change is all that it takes to bring relief.

- Try baby massage (page 90) on a regular basis, or use baby strokes (page 118).

- Carry baby with you in a sling.

- When undressing your baby, try to keep the chest and stomach covered.

- If you think boredom is the problem, move your baby's position or provide a new toy to play with.

- A dummy may provide sucking satisfaction; otherwise a clean mother's knuckle will do.

- Use settling techniques involving rocking, moving, patting or carrying.

How long should I let my baby cry?

This depends on two factors: the level of intensity of your baby's cry and your own tolerance level.

A rule of thumb is: the more intense the cry, the quicker you need to respond.

For example, if your baby's crying is an intermittent grizzle, it's probably best to leave them; they will likely go to sleep this way, and it would be unsettling to pick them up. However, a full-throated, urgent cry needs to be dealt with immediately – if for no other reason than by leaving them, they will work up into an even more fragmented state.

But how about your tolerance level?

A newborn's cries can be very compelling. Nature has designed it that way. But, as your baby matures, you'll learn to distinguish the different types of cries and will feel more comfortable about allowing it occasionally to continue at a low-grade intensity.

Sometimes these cries are simply a way of letting off steam. Your baby may cry as they experience being wrapped for bed, but if you've timed it correctly, this will subside as they move towards sleep. Similarly, they may cry just before attaching to the breast, even refusing it for a moment in frustration. But, by taking your time, this will pass.

There will be times when you feel helpless, or feel your baby's cries represent some sort of failure on your part. Once you accept that all children are different, and that it's perfectly natural for a baby to cry and grumble from time to time, you should feel more at ease. Frustrated, perhaps, but not a failure.

Last-resort procedures

If all attempts at consolation fail, and you feel your baby's crying is becoming too much of a strain for you, it may be time to remove yourself from the scene for a while. This will allow you to rebalance your feelings and you may even find the crying subsides.

- Place baby in bed, or in a safe place, and move somewhere where you cannot hear the cries.
- Employ the Breathing Calm technique (page 61). Continue for at least 5 minutes.
- When you return, apply calming techniques (page 93).

Remember, you cannot force a baby to stop crying. You can only soothe them, then control the way you react to the cries.

Feeding issues

Matters that relate to feeding are at the heart of many a crying incident. If hunger is the problem, feeding is the obvious solution. But, if this has no settling effect, consider the following possibilities:

- If you are breastfeeding, it's impossible to be too relaxed in your approach. Prepare your area in advance. Keep a glass of water or milk nearby, and the television remote control if you so desire. Practise any of the relaxing techniques from this book, particularly the more meditative ones such as Deep Relaxation (pages 58–61).

- Watch the foods you eat. Adult foods such as cabbage, broccoli, as well as stimulants and spices, can have an unsettling effect on a breastfed baby.
- If you are using formula, check the type you are using. Sometimes changing the formula can have an instant settling effect. (Be guided by your paediatrician or mother-care nurse.)
- Experiment with the bottle's nipple size or type – some may have too much or too little milk flow.
- Your baby is not yet efficient at relieving wind themselves, so regular burping throughout a feed is advisable. Most babies respond to upward strokes, taps or rubbing on the back; others respond to being laid on their back and gently moving their legs. Carrying your baby around in a sling may have a similar effect.

Colic

An unexplained crying pattern in a healthy, well-fed infant under three months is commonly referred to as colic. Even though some experts dismiss colic altogether, there is no doubt that its symptoms can present a serious challenge to adult peace of mind and confidence. These symptoms may include:

- crying in the evening after a feed
- baby appears to be in acute distress, with piercing cries
- baby draws their legs up to the stomach in an apparent attempt to relieve abdominal pain
- crying continues for prolonged periods

There are as many theories on dealing with colic as there are on what causes it. One way is to place your baby face-down across your knees and rub their back firmly.

Then there is the 'colic hold' – a way of exerting gentle pressure against the baby's stomach while you carry them around. To do this, let your baby rest along your arm, face-down, with their head near the crook of your elbow. This position appeals to all types of babies, not just those with colic, and can be less stressful on your shoulders and arms than other positions.

Ideally, a colic phase is not something you want to deal with alone as it can be wearing on your nerves. If possible, arrange for your partner or a roster of understanding friends and relatives to support you during these times. If the crying becomes unbearable, use the last-resort procedures (page 95). You may also wish to speak to a child-care professional about other forms of intervention.

The good news is that colic generally passes before you've worked out the best way to deal with it. By about three months, your baby's crying should have diminished to manageable levels.

Making your own life easier

For many women, the months after giving birth can be tiring in the extreme. The massive physical and emotional effort of childbirth gives way to a phase of having to deal with your own regeneration, while fulfilling the constant needs of a new baby.

Although the emotional rewards for this work are many, you may sometimes feel like your life as an individual has vanished. It's quite natural to feel this way; it is the experience of most new mothers at one time or another.

But it is a phase and it will pass. The key to ensuring it passes positively and painlessly is to make adequate time for yourself to relax, recuperate and recharge.

Dealing with physical exhaustion

Broken sleep does more than make you tired. Sleep deprivation has even been used as a form of torture throughout the ages. The stress of it leaves you disoriented, forgetful, incapable of performing more than the simplest tasks, weepy and inclined to mood swings. Sound familiar? In addition to being psychologically disorienting, sleep deprivation also affects your physical wellbeing. In acute cases, it can cause complete physical breakdown.

To understand why it affects you this way, you need to understand the nature of sleep.

- Typically, a night's sleep consists of four or five cycles of 90–120 minutes each. These cycles vary between wakefulness, light sleep and progressively deeper sleep. Within *each* cycle, you experience light sleep, REM (rapid eye movement) or 'dream sleep' and deep sleep.
- During deep sleep, your brain produces deep delta frequencies, indicating that little mental activity is taking place. Your heart rate, blood pressure and rate of breathing are at their lowest levels.

- During REM sleep, your brain is more active. Your heart rate, blood pressure and breathing rate speed up and this is when you dream. Unconsciously you are also working through memories and the issues of the day. Usually REM sleep lasts for about 30 minutes, increasing as the night goes on.
- In addition to this, the patterns of your sleep – when you wake and when you retire – operate to a distinct biological rhythm that is reset each day by sunlight.

If any of these patterns are disturbed in any way, the restorative powers of sleep are greatly diminished. You'll probably feel tired, restless, irritable and unable to think clearly or cope with the normal ups and downs of the day. If you're breastfeeding, you may also experience difficulty producing sufficient milk.

Getting baby to sleep through the night is the holy grail for new parents. But it does happen – with time. While you are waiting for this to happen, invest a little more effort into developing a sense of calm and balance in your own life.

- Use techniques from Chapter 2.
- Let go of the belief that you have to perform certain house-hold duties every day. With the right attitude, it's surprising how long you can postpone these chores without having an adverse effect on your household.
- Learn to sleep when baby sleeps.

Then, if you really feel you need additional energy and focus in your day, cultivate the 'mother napping' technique.

Mother napping

Mother napping is a quick, intense nap that helps improve alertness and state of mind. Nap for 10–20 minutes only. (Longer napping may produce a state known as sleep inertia.) You will find that with practice and confidence, you will easily fall asleep in this time.

- Sit or lie somewhere comfortable.
- Allow yourself to relax thoroughly.
- Tell yourself you will wake at a specific time (use an alarm clock if necessary).
- Clear your mind of all thoughts.
- Allow sleep to envelop you.
- When you wake, sit and relax for a few moments, then get on with your day's activities, feeling rested and energised.

Repeat as many times throughout the day as feels comfortable.

Finding time for yourself

It's easy to find reasons why you shouldn't spare a few minutes for Me Time (page 19) each day. But time spent on yourself is essential for both your state of mind and the wellbeing of your baby.

So, how do you find the time?

The secret is surprisingly simple. Instead of searching for the ideal time, or trying to schedule it into breaks within baby's program, just take it. Say to yourself:

9.00 to 9.30 a.m. [or whatever time you choose] is Me Time.
I will use it for myself, no matter what.

In the early months, when your baby's sleeps are more frequent, you can vary the scheduling of Me Time to take advantage of this flexibility. But this is a temporary solution and, as your baby's sleep patterns become more routine, you will profit by choosing a more regular time each day.

Making the decision to set aside this time is not difficult. Sticking to this decision may be – at least for the first few weeks. After you've experienced it a few times, though, you will begin to appreciate the benefits. You will discover that 30 minutes of Me Time will often be more revitalising than an extra 30 minutes' sleep (assuming, of course, that you've passed through that initial period of sleep deprivation).

Calm is not control

One of the biggest shocks of parenthood – especially for those who are used to getting their own way or have previously lived well-organised lives – is just who's calling the shots now.

It is very human to try to maintain a sense of order in your world. It's also very human to become frustrated when the events of your day do not progress in the orderly fashion you would like.

However, as any physicist will tell you, the natural order of life is chaos. The sooner you accept this, the sooner you will be on the way to becoming calm. Your baby is in control of your schedule right now, and will be for the immediate future. Relax and accept it.

If I could give you just one tip on how to be calm at this time, it would be this: concentrate on doing just one thing at a time. Despite what some people believe, human beings are unable to multi-task effectively. So occupy all of your attention with the task at hand, then move onto the next task when that one is completed. Don't think about the chores that are piling up, just concentrate on the 'now'. Then you can be relaxed about what you're doing and what remains to be done.

Diet and exercise

In the last weeks of pregnancy, you probably started looking forward to the moment when you could get your body back to normal. Then, following the birth, you discover this return to normality is not as immediate as you might have hoped.

You begin to wonder how you will ever get your abdomen to spring back to its former shape. Combine this with a range of physical discomforts you may be experiencing – stitches, soreness, stretch marks, varicose veins, haemorrhoids, hair loss – and you may feel compelled to adopt a rigorous diet and exercise regime right away.

If you rush into vigorous exercise, especially in the first two months, you risk straining the muscles and ligaments that have been softened by hormones in preparation for birth.

In addition, this is hardly the time for strict dieting. You have energy levels to maintain, and your diet has an influence on the well-being of your baby. If you are breastfeeding, you will need to increase your kilojoule intake by around 2000 kj above your pre-pregnancy requirements, as well as increasing calcium and fluids – you should aim to drink at least eight glasses of water a day.

Getting your postnatal body back to its former glory takes time. The best approach is to look at exercise as a relaxed toning regime for the first months. For example, if a walk helps you to switch off and feel invigorated, calm and positive, then walk. Simply going for a stroll with your baby will often be sufficient for the first weeks.

So relax for the moment and consider an easygoing approach to diet and exercise. And if you find you need to improve your self-image in the light of childbirth and lack of sleep, choose one of your favourite activities from Pamper Time (pages 20–21).

Hormonal changes

If ever there was a time when you could blame erratic moods and behaviours on hormones, it's now. Not only are hormones responsible for many of the mood swings during pregnancy, they are often the culprit for mood swings following birth.

Just after delivery, your levels of oestrogen and progesterone drop dramatically. Sometimes this leads to feelings of depression; indeed, 'baby blues' are reported by most women in the first week. So, if you feel weepy and irritable after birth, it's not your fault; it's the hormones.

Postnatal depression (PND), or post-partum depression, is a more pronounced form of these same blues. The indicators for this state range from irritability to suicidal thoughts. It is not unusual to experience one or more of the indicators below, and the fact that you do is not necessarily a cause for alarm. However, be guided by the number, intensity and persistence of these symptoms. If you are concerned, seek assistance from a health-care professional.

Postnatal depression indicators

- overwhelming anxiety, depressed mood and suicidal thoughts
- tearfulness for no reason
- loss of competence and inability to do household tasks
- low self-esteem
- inability to think clearly or find the right words
- exhaustion
- appetite and sleep disorders
- loss of interest in sex
- fear of being alone, or fear of social contact
- irritability
- exaggerated fears about health and safety of self, baby, partner

---

You will note that many of the above indicators also relate to a condition you will have experienced yourself: sleep deprivation.

Indeed, a recent study into women who showed signs of PND found that most improved when their sleeping habits improved or when their babies were encouraged to adopt a more regular sleep pattern.

From newborn to infant: 6 to 18 months

By this stage of a child's development, most parents find they are at last beginning to relax into the parenting role. The stresses that once arose from not knowing what to expect, from night after night of interrupted sleep, and from the inability to fully understand the needs of a tiny baby, are starting to dissipate.

In their place comes a growing familiarity and confidence in what you have to do. And, while tiredness may still be an issue from time to time, all those nights of broken sleep that you endured are slowly becoming a memory.

For most parents, however, this is still a challenging time. What began as a new adventure has now become a job: a round-the-clock routine that seems to offer very little down time or relief.

Fortunately, the relief – and the down time – can be found.

The period from six to 18 months is characterised by major developments in understanding and awareness in your baby. This is an exciting time for the new parent – when your child begins to explore and learn about his or her immediate world.

The world of your baby

Age	Physical development	Mental development	Understanding	Behaviour
6–12 months	Vision almost at adult standard Increasingly mobile (crawling, sliding) May try to stand Adept at using fingers	Has limited memories of experiences Recognises sounds from own language; ignores foreign languages Can recognise self in a photograph or mirror	Understands simple instructions such as 'Don't touch.' Recognises common words Remembers simple events Starts to sort and classify things	Speaks a few words Preference for certain tastes and textures Strives for independence, may reject breast May not be comfortable with strangers Wants all your attention
12–18 months	Walks and climbs Gains weight more slowly, body shape changing Teeth appear Begins to alter daily nap schedule to one per day	Can relate a word to a picture. Remembers simple sequences. Can find hidden objects.	Has a number of words and short phrases in vocabulary Begins to solve simple problems Understands symbolic play	Exerts independence ('No!') Expresses likes and dislikes Imitates adults Throws tantrums Shows pride in accomplishments

This stage also introduces a unique set of pressures for both of you, particularly in relation to your child's **curiosity and mobility**, **dependence** and efforts at **communication**.

Curiosity and mobility

You will notice your child becoming increasingly curious about objects and how to relate to them: picking them up, exploring them with their hands and mouth and, later, organising them by stacking or placing them in a row.

By 10 months or so, your baby is beginning to apply their motor skills with intent: deliberately shaking a rattle to make a pleasing noise, moving an object from the path of something they want, and experimenting with cause and effect by repeatedly dropping things or moving them around.

As these motor skills develop, their explorations widen in scope. Your child's ability to crawl and move into an upright position provides a fascinating new perspective on the world. They may try to crawl under or over large pieces of furniture, to push or drag things around and they are fascinated by everyday temptations such as stairs, cupboards and containers.

This new mobility, coupled with an irresistible drive to extend their boundaries, means babies of this age can easily become a danger to themselves. They can now manoeuvre themselves into a position to explore perilously balanced objects or to push their inquisitive fingers into danger zones such as electrical sockets. Since your child has no concept of what is dangerous, this is the time you need to consider child-proofing your home – unless you want to shadow them everywhere.

This curiosity also leads to frustration. From about 15 months, tantrums may erupt if your child is prevented from exploring the object of their desire, or if they can't work out what to do with some tantalising new item. These outbursts are precursors to the full-blooded tantrums that sometimes beset a two-year-old who is struggling with issues of independence and selfhood.

Dependence

At around seven months, your child may begin to develop a new sense of attachment towards you.

You may begin to see signs of 'stranger anxiety', when your child becomes clingy and protests if handled by someone they don't know, or indeed *anyone* other than mother. The onset of this stage means they will no longer be happy to be passed from one person to another and will start to express clear preferences for certain people.

At the same time, your baby seeks stimulation – their brain is programmed to receive it. They start to search for it themself, but it is not always forthcoming. As your baby is no longer happy to sit quietly and entertain themself, they will expect you to play and to continually present them with different objects, vistas and challenges.

This is more than just a passive desire. Your child can now follow you! Life for you and your baby then enters new territory.

Along with stranger anxiety, your child may sometimes exhibit 'separation anxiety'. They may determinedly shadow your every move, demanding your attention. Even closing a door between you can precipitate tears.

Separation anxiety, like stranger anxiety, sometimes continues throughout the second year, peaking at about 18 months. You may find that the less attention your child receives, the more inclined they are to become upset. Your preference may be to dismiss this; however, in most cases, the more attention you give, the faster they are likely to get over it.

Communication

Because your child now understands some of what you try to communicate, you will naturally expect them to remember certain behaviours or procedures.

Yet, in very young infants, memory exists only in relation to their motor skills; symbolic memory begins to develop later. So your child is unable to appreciate concepts, such as that falling hurts or that a heater is hot, until these messages have been clearly imprinted on their behaviour by experience and repetition.

Cautioning your child with words has little effect. For example, they may know that a certain vase on the table is off-limits. They may even be able to repeat 'No, no' as they approach it, since you have told them this often. But it means little. They don't ignore your instruction in order to be difficult; they simply find the object irresistible.

You will enjoy more success and peace of mind if you decide that rather than expecting your child to remember how they should behave, you simply remove danger and temptation from their path.

Sleep and settling

By this stage you will be endeavouring to teach your child to slide off to sleep by themselves, and to sleep through the night. To begin with, your child will probably wake up every now and then, but the aim is to encourage them to simply turn over and go back to sleep.

The settling techniques from earlier in this chapter may no longer be appropriate because your baby is learning how to move about, pull themselves up and, at around nine months, keep themselves awake when they want to. This means your baby now has an influence on the bedtime process. If they are over-stimulated, or associate bedtime with restlessness or boredom, or decide they need a feed at 3 a.m., they have the potential to upset the sleeping patterns of an entire family.

By six months, your baby has the potential to sleep 10 hours at night. At this stage, they will probably have two sleeps during the day, with the longer one in the morning. Ideally, your child will now be sleeping in a separate room so that parental noises, such as a cough or trip to the bathroom, don't wake them.

At around nine months, you may notice that your baby has become unsettled during the night, even if they have been a relatively good sleeper until now. This relates to their new-found ability to keep themselves awake. Gentle but firm settling techniques should help your child to adjust.

Then, at around 12 months, they may gradually drop the afternoon sleep in favour of an extended one in the morning. The good news is that they have reached the stage where they now sleep soundly through the night, for at least 10 hours. This may be interrupted by periods of restlessness, which is quite common when children begin to walk.

For the sake of the household's harmony and your own rest, it is important to introduce order to your baby's bedtime habits as early as possible.

The calm bedtime

- When you put your child to bed, use the same relaxing procedures, in the same order, every time.
- Speak in a soft voice.
- Avoid stimulating play or activities in the time leading up to bed. Remove entertaining toys from the bed.
- Darken the room and use a night light if necessary.
- If you use rocking or cuddling as a way of making your child sleepy, make sure you put them to bed *before* they fall asleep. The sleep ritual becomes more powerful if your child wakes in the same place they fall asleep.

Freedom to cry

Many parents find that a child's crying is at its most disturbing at bedtime (though not as disturbing as when it occurs at 3 a.m.). What often happens is the child cries strongly, the parent takes them out of bed, attempts to calm them, puts them down again, and then the ritual is repeated again and again. After hours of this, your child will probably fall asleep from sheer exhaustion. Unfortunately, you will share in that exhaustion.

If your child is over seven to eight months, there is a method that some use to establish reasonable sleep patterns. Some call it 'controlled crying' or 'cry it out', both of which sound a bit scary. Let's call it 'freedom to cry'.

If you are convinced that your child's crying is behavioural rather than a sign of illness or discomfort, there may be merit in this procedure. It will only work if your baby has reached the stage when you can leave them alone for short periods of time throughout the day without causing distress. If your child hasn't reached this stage yet, it's too early for this method.

The key to this approach is commitment and consistency on the part of parents. Approach it in the belief that the crying may get a little worse before it gets better. If parents are consistent, most infants show improvement in sleeping habits within a week of commencing this method. But it can be a strain on you, so it's best not to attempt this if you're feeling particularly stressed or fragile yourself.

Freedom to cry involves leaving your infant to cry for progressively longer intervals before entering the room. And, when you do enter the room, it is for progressively shorter intervals. This method effectively assures your child that you are not abandoning them, but conveys the message that you will not get them out of bed.

In itself, this is not what you could call a calm technique – indeed, some parents find it quite distressing – but it may be something you need to employ in order to maintain calm as time goes on.

As freedom to cry can be gruelling, it is important both parents commit themselves to the program and to completing it. If you stop then start again, the message your baby receives will be confused, and all the crying and tension will have been in vain.

Freedom to cry

- Put your child to bed while they are awake but sleepy. Speak gently, stroke your baby, then leave the room.

- If your child cries, re-enter the room after three minutes. Soothe your baby by leaning over, speaking softly and stroking them. Do not lift your child out of bed. And importantly, avoid eye contact. Keep reassuring your child until the intensity of the crying decreases, then leave.

- If your child continues to cry, repeat what you've just done after another three minutes. This time, use your voice, but do not stroke your child.

- Repeat after 5 minutes. Make your visit shorter still. Speak from the doorway so that your child knows you are still around but don't enter the room.

- Repeat after 7 minutes. Make your visit shorter.

- Repeat every 10 minutes until your baby falls asleep.

Vary the above times to what you feel comfortable with. But whatever you do, be consistent.

Note: Don't attempt this method if your child is under seven months old or if they have not reached the stage where you can leave them for short periods without causing distress.

You must also be certain that your child's crying is behavioural rather than a sign that something is wrong. If you have doubts, check with a child-care professional.

If you do embark on this program, it is a good idea to compensate for this drama by spending a bit more cuddling and playing time with your baby during the day.

Calm separations

For many mothers, this stage is the time when child care becomes an issue – when you return to work, or want a little more time to yourself.

Your baby's new quest for independence now begins to pull two ways: towards new horizons as well as towards you. Your child revels in their new-found mobility, but at the same time they make a frightening discovery about you: you can walk away and leave them. Your child may have many new skills, but they are still helpless on their own and will pine for your return.

This is the origin of separation anxiety.

The result is that your child starts to follow you wherever you go. This clashes with *your* independence and occasional need for privacy.

As you are not going to win this struggle in the short term, you might as well just celebrate the fact that someone can't bear to be parted from you. Enjoy the obsession while it lasts. Cultivate your one-handed skills, so you can work or play and still have one hand free for your baby. Leave the door ajar when you are in the bathroom. And postpone things that can't be accomplished with a constant loving stalker to more convenient times.

Of course, there will be times when this constant attention becomes too much. You do need time to yourself. If you can leave your child with your partner, a relative or a friend, this is the time to try it.

But is this parting going to be too much for your child?

Over time, separations can be made less traumatic by ritualising them in such a way that your baby learns to feel secure in your absence – because they know you will return.

Calm separations

- Start with brief absences, then build on them if you need to.
- Each time you leave your child, use the same farewell. The meaning of the words is not as important as the consistency.
- Each time you return, use the same greeting.
- Be consistent with this departing and returning ritual, doing it without fuss or embellishment each time, and your child will come to understand that when you leave them, you always return.

Teething, colds and minor ailments

Teething and other minor ailments can be trying, not just because of the discomforts and possible risks involved for your child, but because they often intensify clinginess, irritability and other behaviours.

Even though the baby teeth are formed at birth, the arrival of the first tooth at about six months is somewhat of a milestone in your child's development. What takes the edge off the celebration is the teething process.

Until recently, many experts believed teething was responsible for everything from sleeplessness to eating disorders, sore ears, excessive drooling, nappy rash and diarrhoea. However, many recent medical studies have shown that there is no correlation between teething and most of the symptoms commonly blamed on it. (This is why it's important not to dismiss symptoms – especially high temperature – as simply 'teething'.)

Whatever symptoms can be blamed on it, there can be no denying that teething is a discomfort for baby and mother.

What can you do about it?

As teething is a natural occurrence that every child goes through, the best you can do is ease the discomfort as much as possible, and to give your baby the love and attention they crave at this time. It's amazing how much you can achieve with a few comforting words and a cuddle.

Teething calm

Relief from teething pain usually comes from pressure, numbing, natural remedies or pain-killers.

- If your baby's gums are not too sensitive, try massaging them with your finger.
- Use a teething gel.
- Use a teething ring. To enhance its effectiveness, leave it in the refrigerator for a while. When baby gnaws on the cold ring, it may numb their gums temporarily. Some teething rings have a special gel inside to retain the coldness.

- Limit the sugar in your child's diet. When sugar combines with the bacteria from your baby's gums, it can create acid which increases discomfort.
- Regularly add a little chamomile tea to your baby's bottle, give it to them on a teaspoon, or soaked in a cold, clean cloth that they can suck on.
- Your child-care professional may also recommend a pharmaceutical or homeopathic remedy.

Six to 12 months is not only the age for teething troubles, it's also when your baby's immune system begins to develop. In addition to behavioural changes such as interrupted sleep, this development is often accompanied by a range of minor infections such as colds, diarrhoea and rashes. Indeed, it is not uncommon for a baby to have six to 10 colds in a year.

From time to time, these minor illnesses cause disturbed sleeping and eating patterns. While you know these usually pass of their own accord, consult a health-care professional if you become concerned, especially if your child is suffering from a high temperature or diarrhoea, which can lead to dehydration. For relief, there are a number of natural, homeopathic or pharmaceutical remedies you may consider.

Above all, times of illness and discomfort demand extra love and attention from you. The following is one way you can impart this comfort and enjoy a relaxing time yourself.

Baby strokes

The Chinese have known for centuries that massaging certain points of the body can bring relief from pain or illness.

Using the lightest brush of your fingertips, try variations on the following when your child is upset:

- With two fingertips of each hand, gently follow the line of your baby's eyebrows as you stroke the brow, around the sides of the head and towards the ears.
- With the gentlest pressure between thumb and forefinger, lightly rub your baby's earlobes.
- Gently rub the soles of baby's feet, especially towards the top near the toes.

Finish or continue according to the feedback your child gives you.

As important as looking after your child's needs during these times is taking care of your own needs. If ever there was a time to indulge yourself with some of the calming routines from this book, it's now.

Baby-proofing your home

After six months, your baby's new inquisitiveness will mean they become irresistibly drawn to stairs, electrical sockets and furniture that can topple. Baby-proofing your home is now an essential step in keeping them out of danger and preserving your own peace of mind.

Firstly, decide where your child is allowed to roam. If baby-proofing your entire home is unrealistic, choose one or two rooms in which they can get about. Make sure that doors to off-limits areas cannot be prised open by determined little fingers. Remember to review your child-proofing mechanisms every few months to cope with your child's new skills.

When all of this is done, your home may not be as elegant as before, but it will be a safe and creative environment for your child.

Peace-of-mind child-proofing

- Begin on your hands and knees so that you can determine the temptation points from a child's point of view.
- Install covers or plastic plugs on all electrical outlets.
- Place all mouth-sized objects out of reach.
- Cover sharp corners of furniture or doorways, remove hanging tablecloths etc.
- Fit gates or doors at the top (and bottom) of staircases.
- Lock away all cleaning products; fit latches where necessary. Keep medicines, herbs and vitamins out of reach. Remove all plastic bags.
- Lock bathroom doors.
- Disconnect appliances and install guards for heaters and fireplaces.
- Check that your house plants are safe for children (many plants are poisonous).
- Finally, compile a readily accessible list of emergency numbers (hospital, doctor, child-care nurse, poison control centre), just in case.

Feeding

Weaning and introducing solids into your baby's diet will probably take place sometime within this period, and is yet another milestone in your baby's development.

Some babies make their own decision to abandon the breast, but the majority need a little coaxing. The most relaxed approach is to make weaning a gradual process – this minimises the effect of milk-engorged breasts for you, and any feelings of abandonment or rejection for baby.

It's probably best to initiate this when there are no other pressures in your life. Not only can weaning generate another period of clingy and unsettled behaviour in your child, you both have to come to terms with baby eating solids.

Feeding solids to a baby does wonderful things to your tolerance for mess. The solution? Learn to live with it. Part of the learning experience of eating solid foods is exploration – with fingers, hands and sometimes even the mouth!

This introduction to solids also ushers in new opportunities for power plays between baby and mother. Now your child can not only throw, squish, mash and play with their food, they can reject it altogether. If your baby decides to use meal times as an arena to explore their independence, it may be best to look on it as a temporary set-back and simply ensure that they eat something nourishing at each sitting.

One strategy you could try is to remove the food altogether and give the child a toy or something to distract them. Later, calmly reintroduce the food. If your child still refuses, offer something you know they like. Many children prefer smaller, more frequent snacks anyway.

Experiment with small amounts of different foods with different textures. Try cutting or arranging it in different ways – perhaps with a little humour and imagination. You may also find your child prefers to feed themself.

As your child approaches two years of age, there may be even more changes in their tastes and eating habits. The food they loved yesterday, they loathe today. Generally, though, your child will eat if really hungry and this pickiness will become less pronounced.

Of course, if you suspect your child is ill or not receiving adequate nutrition, check with your child-care professional.

Re-establishing your identity

After the first six to eight months (or a little longer if you're breast-feeding), you may start to feel that you've just about come through a long tunnel. You sense that after all those months of being isolated, you can now begin to look outward once again.

But things are not as they used to be. Whether you like it or not, your life is no longer entirely your own. Moreover, what you are experiencing is quite different from a conventional partnership of give and take and mutual support; this new relationship demands your time, energy and commitment every day.

At the same time, you may find that your relationship with your partner has changed. To a degree, this is to be expected. Relationships are often put on hold while you come to grips with the more pressing demands of motherhood. There is nothing unusual about this.

You may also find you have a different feeling about your body – about how it looks and feels. Sometimes this means sexual intimacy takes a back seat to the more pressing physical need for sleep.

All these are normal changes which most new mothers experience to some degree. Whether you view them as positive or negative depends entirely on your perspective. You can resent the changes, or you can use them as an opportunity to redefine yourself within a family context. Indeed, this can be a time to *improve* your relationships. Many couples find parenthood to be a time of growth and bonding – especially when there is a sharing of roles.

So have a little fun. Re-explore your relationship with your partner. Plan on a candle-lit dinner after baby has gone to bed. Choose your best outfit. Hide all the baby stuff. Indulge in a bottle of your favourite wine.

This is a time to turn your attention to yourself, and perhaps your partner, and enjoy a little pampering. Consider whatever little luxuries you can afford. You've earned them. A new outfit, hairstyle, facial, aromatherapy oils, yoga, new exercise regime or, most important of all, some time for yourself. You may want to visit the library, go to the gym, stroll in the park, call on some friends or just sit in a coffee shop by yourself for a hour or so. This is your own time – enjoy it.

This pampering is more than an indulgence for you. Soon your baby will enter an extremely active phase during which they will test your energy and patience levels even more. You will find it easier to cope with this when you're feeling relaxed, confident and supported. Remember, **a happy, contented parent more often than not has a happy, contented child.**

Isolation and building networks

One of the side effects of modern life, especially if you live in a big city, is isolation from other people. Some mothers can feel very distant from other people, especially if they spend a lot of time at home looking after a young child. Within this context, everyday problems can loom disproportionately large. But you are not alone in your experiences and frustrations.

One of the most rewarding things you can do at this time is to link up with a network of others in similar circumstances. Join a playgroup or an informal babysitting club, where participants take turns minding each other's children. This way you can occasionally get a chance to spend time on your own without having to factor in the cost of a babysitter. Even if the only thing you have in common with others is your children, such networks can be worthwhile sources of insight and support. In addition, playgroups enable children of similar ages to make their first social interactions, supervised and supported by you.

The contact point for these groups can often be found at the local baby clinic or child-care centre, or through the local maternity hospital. If you can't find such a group in your area, start one of your own.

Toddler power: 18 to 36 months

The dominant theme of the toddler phase is exploration. Your child now has an irresistible urge to push the limits of their abilities and, in doing so, the limits of your patience.

Prepare yourself for a time of contrasts. One moment your child will be the epitome of charm, the next they will be frustrating in the extreme. But this toddler phase doesn't need to be all about stress and tantrums; it's also time for a bit of calm for both of you.

The world of your toddler

Age	Physical	Mental	Understanding	Behaviour
18–36 months	Legs and trunk lengthen; looks more like a child than a baby Play becomes more complex Distinct preferences for certain foods and activities	Begins to grasp concepts and ideas Becomes upset when separated from loved ones Can recall different places and environments	Good language skills Understands most things you say Can follow two-step instructions like 'Go to the chair and get dolly.' Develops preferences for other children	Sleeps through the night Learning quickly Enjoys learning new skills Strives for independence, yet wholly dependent Demanding

Your toddler's developing mobility and curiosity mean they will still occasionally be a danger to themself. And because your child now sleeps less, probably taking just one nap during the day, they have more time for play and mischief. However, your toddler's ability to learn is still intimately bound up with their motor skills, through experience and repetition.

For many mothers, the defining characteristic of this stage relates to dependence – or independence. On one hand, your toddler is driven to test their boundaries and capabilities. On the other, they are plagued by feelings of insecurity when separated from you.

The tension between these two extremes can be tiring for everyone. From your toddler's point of view, if you limit their desire for independence, you frustrate them and they become angry. Then, if you attempt to reduce their clinginess in any way, you encourage feelings of insecurity.

In addition, your child is continually wrestling with emotions and competency levels they don't understand. They become frustrated by tasks that are beyond them, and sometimes by their own short attention span. They still cry on occasion and they are now beginning to understand the effect this has on you. Your toddler may push, bite, scratch and break things without intentionally setting out to harm or cause damage; after all, they don't have the ability to view these actions from someone else's perspective. Then, just when you thought you'd never really understand the meaning of these actions, out pops a new word.

This emerging ability to communicate is perhaps your child's most important social achievement yet. By two and a half, your toddler will probably be babbling fluently, with a vocabulary of a number of identifiable words and phrases.

Another advance is also occurring at this stage: your toddler begins to think symbolically. You may observe the first glimpses of this in the way they order their thoughts. For example, they start to remember where they placed an object or what they were doing in the past. They are probably able to grasp general concepts such as 'in' and 'out'.

But the word they embrace over and above all others is 'no'. This becomes the most overused word in the mother–toddler lexicon. When you direct it towards your child, you suspect they understand the meaning even if they don't respond to it. But when they direct it towards you, there is no doubt. When they say 'No' it becomes a powerful statement of their independence, and some children flaunt this independence more readily than others.

This is the time for you to start thinking about **positive versus negative instruction**.

Positive versus negative instruction

Everyone feels more relaxed about saying yes than no. You know from experience that it is a lot less stressful to respond in the positive than the negative, no matter what your opinion of a situation. And for more people, a positive instruction ('Walk around the table') is much more motivating than a negative one ('Don't walk into the table').

You may conclude that there's no point losing any sleep over this issue now, since your toddler's understanding of language won't yet accommodate such subtlety. But it's never too early to start concentrating on the positive – for your sake as well as your child's.

You will find life becomes more harmonious for both of you if you concentrate on encouraging positive behaviours rather than trying to correct negative ones.

There's no point in trying to prevent your toddler from doing what they are naturally programmed to do. Toddlers need to climb, empty things out and try to fill them again, as well as experiment with shapes, tastes and textures. Your best action is to provide an environment where they can constructively pursue these ends.

If you don't want your child to climb on your new sofa, direct them towards an alternative that they can climb on. Since you won't want your toddler to splash water over your freshly cleaned carpet, urge them to do it in the bathroom. If you'd rather your toddler didn't rush headlong towards the stairs, encourage them to expend their energy in a baby-proofed room.

Calm comes, not from limiting your child's natural exuberance, but from directing it positively.

Tantrums

At this stage your child is also beginning to come to grips with their own emotions. As well, they often feel frustrated because they are unable to communicate their wishes or intentions effectively. Combine these two factors and you have the formula for a temper tantrum – quite common for children between the ages of 18 and 36 months.

There are three things you can be relatively sure of with a tantrum at this age.

- It will catch you by surprise. One moment your toddler is relaxed and charming, the next they are crying or screaming.
- It will be over equally as unexpectedly.
- It is seldom manipulative in intent.

Tantrums are unpleasant experiences for everyone involved, particularly the child. Although your toddler may appear wilful, the loss of control involved in a tantrum can be quite frightening for them. This is why it's important for you to respond in a calm but firm fashion.

In the first chapter, we explored how emotional states can be transferred from one person to another. A tense person spreads tension, while a calm person spreads calm. However, in the case of tantrums, this is not always so.

Yes, it's true that a tense person does spread tension. If you respond angrily to your child's tantrum, it achieves little more than displaying how adults can lose control just like children. This can intensify your toddler's difficult behaviour.

However, in this case, the converse isn't always so. A calm approach doesn't always produce an immediate calming effect, because tantrums are a form of hysteria that need to peak before they subside.

Once the tantrum has passed, your child should recover to find that all is safe and well in the world, and that this behaviour has attracted neither reward not punishment. Calmly discuss what has just happened; acknowledge your child's frustration, explain that you appreciate something was not to their liking or that you failed to understand what they were trying to convey. The purpose of this is not just restoring empathy, it is demonstrating that words and language are the favoured vehicle of communication, rather than hysterical acts.

If a tantrum happens while you're in a public place, the first step is to quickly adjust *your* thinking. Tell yourself that when the screaming starts, the onlooking world will neatly divide into two groups. One group will have experienced what you're going through and be sympathetic; the other group will blame you for what's going on. On one side are your peers; on the other are those who will never understand the ups and downs, the magic and ordeals of parenthood.

Take strength from your peers! Give them a shrug and a smile – they will empathise. Ignore everyone else – they will never understand. But under no circumstances allow yourself to be embarrassed into overreacting or to giving in to your child's unreasonable demands. You know that threatening or bullying will get you nowhere, and bribery only encourages repeated behaviour, so it's best to concentrate on your tantrum management in as calm and dignified a way as possible.

Managing a tantrum

- Remember that your child is as disturbed by their behaviour as you are.
- Remain calm, neutral and firm about how you respond.
- Contain your toddler so they do minimal damage to themself or the environment. Remove all dangerous or vulnerable objects from their reach. If in a public place, head for a changing room or somewhere less populated.

- Either sit with your child or hold them in a firm embrace. Alternatively, quietly leave the room briefly, telling them you will return in a few minutes. (Take care not to let them think they're being abandoned.)
- Give comfort afterwards, but take care not to seem to be rewarding their behaviour.
- Calmly discuss what happened, so your child can see how words and language are a preferable way to communicate.

Possibly the best strategy for handling tantrums is the pre-emptive one. If you know what environments or activities usually produce tantrum behaviour in your child, try to avoid them altogether. If you know it often happens when your child is hungry, take a small, secret food item with you for just that eventuality. Sometimes it helps to have a choice of food items, which affords a little extra distraction as well.

If your child is inclined to become agitated when moved between one activity (such as play) and another (such as a bath), pre-empt the second activity. Give them plenty of warning that the second activity is going to happen shortly, so they have time to adjust.

If you believe your child's tantrums occur more frequently than is reasonable, it may be an indication that your toddler is stressed over some issue or another. Have you given them too many rules to deal with at this stage? Is your toddler starting child care or reacting to a new baby in the house? Are *you* showing signs of stress – and are they reacting to that? Any one of these factors can encourage negative behaviour in a toddler.

Sleep disturbances

Now that you have more or less passed through the stage when your baby interrupts your sleep, you enter the stage when they have the ability to disrupt their own. It is not unusual for a degree of sleep resistance to occur in children at the toddler phase, even if they have been sleeping without difficulty before. Often this is simply asserting their independence now that they have the ability to keep themself awake. Other times it may be due to the surges in their development and the tensions inherent in this.

A certain amount of grumbling and noise is part of every toddler's behaviour. And, while it may sometimes be disturbing or annoying for you, it may be more effective to leave them to work it out themself rather than for you to intercede. Naturally, the intensity of your toddler's noise-making is the key, though, by this stage, you'll be familiar enough with their various sounds to know if they have a problem or not.

At around two years old, some toddlers experience night terrors. These are different to nightmares in that they usually occur about an hour after your toddler falls asleep and are characterised by fear, rapid heartbeat, and sometimes sweating and shaking. Often your child will not be fully awake and will resist comforting for some time. However, once this has passed, they will quickly return to sleep and won't remember a thing in the morning.

Nightmares, on the other hand, are often remembered a little longer. Your child may be able to describe certain events or images in a dream (if their linguistic skills allow), and it may take longer to resettle them afterwards. Also, nightmares usually occur about halfway through the night.

So what can you do to prevent your child from experiencing night terrors or nightmares? Very little. The best you can do is ensure bedtime is calm and routine, and that your child endures as little stress as possible. (And a cuddly toy in bed doesn't hurt.)

New siblings

The arrival of a new baby in the family is always an interesting complication in the life of a toddler. In the first instance, your toddler is hardly mature enough to accept that Mum might have a new focus, and will probably be tired and unable to attend to them exclusively. Secondly, your toddler will struggle to come to grips with the concept that they need to consider another person as well as themself. This naturally leads to a degree of jealousy and hurt, as well as the love–hate tension we know as sibling rivalry.

Sometimes these tensions lead to increased tantrum behaviour, problems with sleeping, eating and relating, and perhaps heightened aggression. Your toddler is not just being temperamental out of jealousy; they can neither understand the emotions they are experiencing nor communicate them adequately. Importantly, this is not a behaviour you have to correct.

Besides, after the first few months, your toddler is unlikely to even remember a time before having a little brother or sister. Infants are extremely adaptable; if they are given their basic emotional quotient of attention, the spectre of sibling rivalry can usually be avoided.

This is not to suggest that your task will be easier. Managing a newborn as well as the fragile emotions of a toddler at the same time is quite a task. Some child-care workers say that such a combination is even more difficult than raising twins. However, there are a number of steps you can take to ensure your toddler accepts a new baby in as positive a way as possible.

Introducing a new baby

- Talk to your toddler and show them books about families with new babies well before the birth.
- Introduce your child to their unborn sibling once they can feel the baby moving.
- Involve your toddler in discussion about baby names, what will happen, and what a baby does. A doll may help you illustrate these points.
- Introduce new carers or new child-care arrangements well in advance so there is time for your toddler to adjust.
- Make secure arrangements for your toddler – arrange carers and environments they are familiar and comfortable with – for the weeks surrounding the birth. If you're packing yourself a bag for hospital, pack one for your toddler as well.
- Encourage hospital visits when you're feeling well and cheerful. Allow your toddler to hold the baby (with your help).
- Try to do the same activities with your toddler after the birth as you did before. Let them be a baby again from time to time. Avoid breastfeeding in front of them for the first days.
- Don't expect your toddler to love the baby immediately, but encourage their participation and help.
- Most important of all, take care not to compare siblings.

Toilet training

Now comes the moment you've been thinking about for the past year or so: the day when you no longer have to change nappies. But how do you know when it's time to start toilet training?

It's widely accepted today that it should be the child who determines when the time has come, not you. There is no point in trying to force it before they are ready; after all, you don't want this to become an exercise in tension and anxiety.

Signs of being ready include a broad understanding of what is desired, the ability to understand basic instructions, the ability to remain dry for at least two hours at a time, as well as the willingness to exert independence.

If you attempt to train your toddler too early, the result will be inconsistency – some days it will work, others it won't – and the sense of failure this produces can be counterproductive. It may be much easier to persist with nappies a while longer rather than stalking your child, potty in hand, all day long.

Before about 24 months, a child is generally powerless to consistently get to the potty in time. Even after that stage, accidents will occasionally happen. However, there's no harm in introducing the potty earlier on, simply for its interest value. It's just another household object they can acquaint themself with.

Another timing consideration is the weather. Some mothers claim that the only time for toilet training is summer because of the ease of removing clothing and cleaning up after a mishap. Also, it makes sense not to attempt this process in circumstances that are out of the norm – such as on holidays or when the normal routine of your household is disrupted.

Toilet training can be a rewarding time for your child, bringing with it a great sense of accomplishment. But it is very much a two-steps-forward, one-step-back process. Some days you win; some days you lose. As long as you're heading in the right direction, you can relax.

Calm toilet training

- Wait until the time is right.
- If possible, train in summer.
- Try not to push too hard; patience pays off for both of you.
- Be as delighted with your child's successes as they are.
- Expect accidents, and keep plenty of cleaning-up equipment at hand.
- If it all gets too much on any occasion, pull out the nappies for a few days and relax.

Allowing choice

Just as adults respond badly to having all their decisions made for them, so do children. If for no other reason than to encourage positive behaviour, it is essential for a child to be able to make their own choices occasionally – or to *feel* they are making their own choices.

Put yourself in your child's position. Which of the following would make you feel like drinking your milk?

'Would you like cold milk or hot milk?'

Or 'Drink your milk!'

Your toddler will feel more inclined to take your offer on board if you place it in the context of a choice.

You decide what the choices are, your child makes the choice.

Choice for your child

Children are more compliant and feel more relaxed, if they feel they are making their own choices. If your child is difficult with food, for example, offer a choice of two food items that are acceptable to you: 'Would you like the carrots or the potato?'

If your toddler doesn't want to put on their shoes, give them a choice: 'Would you like the red shoes or the white ones?'

If your child refuses to put down Teddy and have a bath, give them a choice: 'Would you like Teddy to watch you in the bath, or would you rather he had a rest for a little while?'

There's no guarantee of success, but your chances of getting your way are greatly improved when choice is offered.

Moderating your child's behaviour

Now that your child has reached the stage of starting to exert their independence, you might explore your own attitudes towards discipline and the management of toddler behaviour.

Even though it is unlikely that children of this age would be capable of manipulative forethought, some parents are convinced they will attempt to wield power over them if not kept in line. This inevitably leads to parent–child power struggles that can continue all the way through adolescence and beyond.

Underpinning this tension is the notion that children are somehow the property of their parents and should be grateful for the sacrifices parents make for them. These are issues that may never consciously enter your mind, yet still govern the way you react when your toddler attempts to establish their individuality.

In determining their boundaries, your child will make a mess, throw tantrums, refuse to eat their food, display aggressive behaviour and get themself into dangerous situations. But at the same time as they insist on doing things for themself, they will protest if you walk off and leave them to it.

Your reaction to this behaviour will be determined by your attitude towards discipline. Do you believe discipline should relate to controlling bad behaviour? Or should it relate to encouraging more acceptable behaviour?

A parent who favours the former will tend to use discipline as a punishment or as a deterrent for bad behaviour. To be successful, this negative approach depends on fear.

A parent who favours the other approach – encouraging more acceptable behaviour – will use discipline as a way of setting limits, and being consistent and firm. This is positive discipline.

While the negative approach will often produce faster results, it can also produce a more negatively oriented person in the future. On the other hand, a positive approach to discipline not only produces more positive short-term behaviour, it encourages a more positive, happy state of mind in the future.

In any event, punishment only works when a child is mature enough to learn the lesson and keep it in mind for the future. Generally, this would not be the case until your child is 36 months or older. Using punishment before that age generally only succeeds in teaching your child to fear adults.

Time out

Many parents believe 'time out' is an effective form of discipline for young children.

As a form of punishment, time out is usually ineffective because a toddler will not understand its intent or relevance – especially if used as a way of dealing with emotional outbursts. Even if they do understand, their attention span is such that they usually forget what brought on this punishment in the first place.

Used positively, however, time out can be an effective way of helping your child learn to cope with their frustrations and to calm down in an emotionally charged situation.

If you decide to use this technique, try not to ritualise it as a way of dealing with problems – at least not until your child is older and understands the relationship between their behaviour (the cause) and your reaction to it (the effect).

There's no doubt that the major beneficiary of time out is you.

It allows you a break from the crisis, to remove yourself from the struggle and to wait for the outburst to subside.

Fortunately, there is a more positive alternative to the traditional approach. I call it Calm Time Out. Its purpose is to induce calm in your child and to allow guilt-free breathing space for you.

Calm Time Out

To be effective, Calm Time Out must be associated with becoming calm. There is no room for anger, fear or hostility. Be wary of associating it with punishment, especially if your child is under 36 months, as they probably won't understand its intent or meaning.

- Go to your Calm Space (see pages 54–55) if possible.
- Speak slowly in a soft voice. Slow down all your gestures and movements. Slow down your breathing as well.
- Gradually introduce your toddler to the concept of having Calm Time Out from stressful behaviour. To begin with, stay with your child the whole time, perhaps sharing in a distracting experience such as reading a book. Later, you will be able to leave them in another room.
- Let your child understand that the purpose of Calm Time Out isn't punishment, but a way of allowing both of you to calm down.
- Remind your toddler that there is no hurry, that you are allowing them whatever time they need to relax and become calm. (Use words like this even if your child doesn't immediately understand them – they will grasp the meaning.) ▶

- Neither pay too much attention to what your child is doing nor try to console them at this time. Simply allow them to work through their own emotions.
- Never lock the door.

In spite of how effective Calm Time Out may be, the pre-emptive alternative should also be part of your calming repertoire.

To do this, you simply encourage positive behaviour more often than you correct negative behaviour. Be effusive with your praise of good behaviour, and make a habit of explaining more positive ways of dealing with the situations your toddler may encounter. ('Now let's see if there's a better way of moving these toys out of your way.') Steer your child towards positive activities that are a better alternative to the negative ones which lead to their frustration.

Challenging your own views

There is a huge difference between misbehaviour and what a toddler does out of natural inquisitiveness. Accepting this difference means you may sometimes have to question your own reactions and motives.

It is perfectly normal for a mother to become angry and frustrated at the behaviour of her child. Every mother goes through this at some time.

How you react to these emotions is what turns the situation into a positive or negative experience.

Given your choices, you would always want to react positively rather than negatively; you would rather your child saw you as balanced and fair-minded rather than loud and ill-tempered. What mother wouldn't?

But in times of high stress, your choices will seem more limited. The more pressure you feel, the more likely it is that your reactions will be negative rather than positive.

Conversely, when you are calm, more options will seem possible. You will see positive ways of dealing with situations that, in another frame of mind, you might think were difficult or impossible. And when you feel calm, your child will be more inclined to feel calm as well.

True, you do have to work at it, but becoming calm is enjoyable work. Practise a few techniques from this book. Look for their pleasurable side. Make them part of your everyday. And, as you grow calmer, you'll be surprised at how much more positive and cooperative your child will become.

The older child: 3 to 5 years

Until recently, you would have thought of yourself and your baby as a unit; after all, that is the way your baby has been thinking, and that's probably the way you've felt because of the round-the-clock demands of your role. But all this is about to change.

The world of your young child

Age	Physical development	Mental development	Understanding	Behaviour
3–5 years	Grows rapidly Height increases faster than weight Masters activities such as running, hopping, throwing a ball Tests physical skills and courage No afternoon nap	Can entertain two emotions at the same time May develop imaginary playmates	Sees themself as an individual Can communicate feelings and ideas Vocabulary of several hundred words Has a concept of the recent past and immediate future	Increased attention span Talks incessantly; asks many questions Plays with friends and is learning how to share May like to choose own clothes

Your young child is now growing rapidly. They may appear thinner than you've been used to as their height is increasing faster than their weight. This is accompanied by a new physical confidence – they can run, hop, throw a ball, climb stairs and may occasionally want to test their physical skills and courage.

Bit by bit, the quest for independence has become a central part of your child's development. Now your child is beginning to see themself as the individual they've become. With an extensive vocabulary, they can communicate much of what they are feeling or thinking – even abstract ideas.

Many of the personality, and even behavioural, traits you are seeing now will remain with your child in some form throughout their life.

Also, many of their broad likes and dislikes will start to evolve into a long-term pattern. This is an exciting time in your child's development.

At the same time, you will be experiencing changes yourself. As well as growing in confidence as a parent, you may be thinking about the new responsibilities looming. You'll be aware of the increasing number of choices your own life is beginning to offer now that your child is not so dependent. You can afford more time to yourself. You can imagine a time when your child will be at school, and you'll be able to pursue your own needs and wants more fully.

However, one of the most significant changes you will go through is the evolution from appendage to role model. Until now, your child has mimicked your behaviour in a superficial sense, but now they will start to copy aspects of your personality, your likes and dislikes and your values.

If ever there was any truth in the assertion that calm parents produce calm children, it starts to show now. This is the ideal time to practise the Calm Role (page 35).

Whether we're talking about being calm, about being thoughtful and civil, or about any aspect of behaviour at all, you are now the most influential role model for your child's development.

Calm suggestion

When it comes to guiding your child through the pitfalls of life, you'll eventually arrive at the realisation that you will often be ignored. The fact that you say something is no guarantee that it will be heeded.

Now that your child is beginning to test their independence, and will continue to do so throughout their life, it's time to explore the difference between instruction and suggestion.

Often the difference between being persuasive (in sales, politics or therapy) and less so is simply understanding the difference between instruction and suggestion.

If you want someone to respond to your request, suggestion is more persuasive than instruction. In both cases, your intent is the same; the difference is the words you use and the way you use them.

Instruction is when you tell someone to do something. For example, 'Pick up your toys.' If your child is cooperative, you will get your way; but their cooperation depends on either *willingness* to please, or *fear* of what will happen if they refuse.

This will usually work when a child is very young, but their resistance to instruction increases as they grow older. Indeed, there are certain phases – such as around the ages of five, seven, nine and adolescence – when instruction is a good way of producing the opposite reaction to the one you want.

Suggestion is more persuasive. Suggestion is when you plant an idea in somebody's head so that they choose to follow a certain course of action of their own accord. They feel happier about doing what you suggest. For example, if you want your child to pick up their toys, you might try a suggestion like: 'Wouldn't you like to help Mummy now and pick up your toys?' Or, 'Wouldn't you like the room to be all neat and tidy before Grandma comes, after you pick up your toys?'

Suggestions such as these are persuasive because this is the way most people prefer you to communicate with them. There is no deception. Your request is straightforward and the words you use imply choice rather than command.

This way of formulating your speech becomes more powerful still when you combine it with imagery. For example, 'Imagine how neat this room is going to look when you pick up your toys.' Or, 'How big do you think the smile on Mummy's face will be when you pick up your toys?'

Depending on the age of the person you're speaking to, you may sometimes have to combine both forms of communication – suggestion as well as instruction. However, use instruction as a last resort. Start with suggestion.

Calm suggestions

The characteristics of a calm suggestion are:

- It usually combines two thoughts in the one suggestion. The first thought is usually one that is easy to agree to, for example, 'How big do you think the smile on Mummy's face will be . . . ?' The second thought is really a simple instruction: 'when you *pick up the toys*'.
- Use positive language for both.
- Combine imagery with your suggestion to make it doubly effective. 'Imagine how neat this room is going to look . . . '
- Depending on the age of the person you're speaking to, you may sometimes have to combine both forms of communication. In this situation, use this simple formula: start with suggestion, resort to instruction.

By the way, you are probably already using calm suggestions quite unconsciously. Every time you smile broadly when you ask your child to drink their milk, you are making a suggestion: that by drinking their milk, they please you. If you do this repeatedly, your child will learn that drinking their milk produces a favourable response and they will be more likely next time to choose this option.

Relaxation time

Today there's a very blurry line between stimulation and relaxation. Indeed, many people now seek stimulation for their relaxation. They seek out more and more novel forms of exciting activities in this quest.

But let's not fool ourselves. Stimulation is the *opposite* of relaxation. Stimulation is designed to excite and titillate the senses and nervous system. Relaxation, on the other hand, works to soothe them. Stimulation excites; relaxation calms.

Nowhere is this difference more important than in the lives of young children.

The pressure to provide more and more stimulating activities for your child comes from all directions – from television, computer games promoters, radio, magazines, other adults and the children themselves. Underpinning this pressure is the subtle suggestion that if you're not providing sufficient stimulation for your children, you're doing them a disservice.

Think of where this could lead.

Even the most limited scenario has the television set as a major influence in a child's life. Imagine all your human values being shaped by the Cartoon Network! Look around most homes and you'll see the TV is joined by a proliferation of computers, video games, board games and electronic toys.

Taking this concept to the extreme leads to a phenomenon known as 'hot-housing', where small children go from one personal development program to the next, every day of the week – today ballet, tomorrow piano, Wednesday judo, Thursday soccer, Friday elocution, and so on.

While a child's development does depend on stimulation, their day does not have to be filled with it. *In*activity is a critical part of their mental and emotional development. In other words, your child needs time to relax – not just before bedtime, but many times throughout the day. Your child's nervous system depends on this, and is built to expect it. Only relaxation helps a child's body and mind calm down after stimulating activities. Further stimulation – even if it's simply watching TV – denies the nervous system this chance to rebalance.

Allow your child the opportunity to relax throughout the day – so they can have moments of stillness when they are encouraged to enjoy quiet times by themself. Unstructured moments such as sitting in the garden staring at the progress of a snail, fantasising about the secret life of a plaything, or staring at their reflection in the window can be the most calming of all.

Food

You will have noticed by now that certain foods affect your child in different ways. The negative effects of dietary imbalances are fairly obvious. These effects include:

- weight problems
- tooth decay
- lack of energy
- mood swings
- behavioural issues

As well as knowing the adverse effects, you probably also know many of the foods that are responsible: processed foods, refined sugar, chocolate, saturated animal fats, food dyes and artificial preservatives and caffeine-intensified beverages. Simply by limiting the quantity of potentially offending foods in a child's diet, you can have a positive effect on their mood and general health.

Listed below are foods that tend to make children more tense and fidgety, and, in extreme cases, hyperactive:

- **Processed foods:** Most processed foods have questionable nutritional value and, depending on the base product and the additives, may sap energy.
- **Refined sugar:** Produces energy for children, but at the expense of mood. Sugar is blamed for suppressing the immune system and has strong mood-altering effects: it elevates then depresses. The 'empty calories' of refined sugar are of no benefit. In addition, sugar is known as an anti-nutrient – one that

depletes your levels of essential nutrients such as zinc, chromium and vitamins B3 and B6. Bear in mind that a well-nourished child does not crave sweets.

- **Artificial preservatives:** These can produce a range of negative health and mood effects. For example, sulfites (which you'll find in foods such as canned tuna) are known to produce food allergies and asthma in some people.
- **Additives:** Depending on the additive, these can produce a range of negative health and mood effects. For example, monosodium glutamate (MSG) – the flavour enhancer you find in so many processed foods – sometimes affects the nervous system of children and adults, producing a variety of effects ranging from mood swings to anxiety attacks and depression.
- **Caffeine-intensified foods:** This not only includes cola, but chocolate, fizzy drinks and many sweets. One can of cola consumed by a small child is the equivalent of eight espresso coffees for a grown man! Caffeine encourages nervousness, restlessness and insomnia.

So the first step is to limit these mood-altering foods and then replace them with calm foods. Refer back to Chapter 2 for details on the Calm Diet (pages 43–50).

Of course, there's no need to get alarmist about all of this. A sensible, well-balanced diet is usually all it takes to keep children on an even keel. However, if you believe your child would enjoy being a little calmer, consider the following steps to calm nutrition.

- Lead by example. Your child is influenced by what you do and how you eat, more so than any dietary advice or instruction offered.

- Start early. Lifetime eating habits begin at the earliest age. Help your child cultivate a taste for fruits and vegetables, and they will be less attracted to the big flavours of packaged products.

- Use healthy foods and snacks as a reward rather than sweets. Have healthy snacks in the house – fresh or dried fruits, cheese, wholegrain crackers, sliced vegetables, yogurt, salsa, dips. Also, if you arrange your pantry or refrigerator in such a way that only the good foods are within reach, guess which ones they will choose first.

- Consider 'gift-wrapping' healthy foods, such as an apple or banana, in a paper bag to make it more like a treat.

- Feed your child often. Most children need healthy snacks at least a couple of times a day. If your child becomes irritable in the afternoons, this is often an indication that their blood sugar level is low and they need nourishment.

- Use milk as a calming food.

Sleep

Now that your child has dispensed with the daytime nap and is more or less settled into a nightly sleeping routine, you may start to think you've seen the end of your struggles. Then again, maybe you haven't.

You've probably discovered by now that the bedtime story is

a great way to unwind – both for chi...
of Mum or Dad's voice relating the s...
child into a relaxed, sleepy state.

Sometimes, however, this is not enou...
are quite common for children in this ag...
a calm bedtime ritual (page 111) and trie...
your child still won't nod off to sleep, try te...

This involves telling a long story in a calm...
words such as 'sleep', 'rest', 'weary eyes' and '...
surprised at the psychological effect they can ha...

If you can't think of a story, try a variation on t... ...g (alter
it according to the gender and interests of your ch... ...s story is
laced with sleep suggestions that most children can't ... . Have fun
with it!

...arent. Usually the sound ...takes to coax your ...sleep patterns ...created ...but

---

The sleep story

Slow Moe could hardly wait for the day to end.
Bedtime was his very favourite time.

Just after he would go to bed, he'd **start to have
wonderful, wonderful dreams.** Sometimes in his dreams he would
be on a pirate ship, sailing across the wide open oceans, rocking
from side to side, looking for adventure.

Sometimes he would be a jet pilot, flying his gleaming white
aircraft through the clouds. Whenever he would pass through the

sky. He'd **float through the sky, feeling**

clouds he'd se_~~ _ould_ be riding a beautiful white horse. He'd
peaceful_~~_ with the breeze on his face and **not a care in**

_~~e_ **closes his eyes, Slow Moe is in a dream.** Once his
_~~_ never knows what he is going to do next.

_~~_ these adventures make Slow Moe **soooo tired.** Whether
~~ing or standing or **lying comfortably in his soft bed, he is so**
tired.

No matter what time it is, Slow Moe **wants to fall asleep.**

He is **so weary,** he yawns all through breakfast.

His mother looks at him and asks, 'Why are you yawning?'

But he can't think of anything to say because **his eyes feel so
sleepy.**

'Slow Moe,' she says, '**why are you yawning?**'

'It's a dream,' says Slow Moe. '**I close my eyes** and I start to
dream. Every time. Last night I was an astronaut, flying through
space – I could go anywhere I wanted to.'

'That's why **you're so tired,**' his mother says, 'and why **you feel
like sleeping right now.**'

At school, when Moe should be listening to his teacher, he finds
himself **yawning again.**

'**Why are you yawning?**' asks the teacher. 'Are we keeping you
from bed, Moe?'

'Sorry Miss,' Moe replies. '**I close my eyes** and I start to dream.

Every time. Last night I was an angel **sitting on a cloud, floating through the sky.** I floated wherever the breeze took me.'

'That's all well and good, Moe,' said the teacher, 'but please try to get more sleep. **You seem very, very tired.**'

After school Moe and his friends ride their bikes to the park. Moe wants to go on the slide but he is **so tired he can hardly move his arms and legs. They feel so heavy.** Even **his hands feel heavy.** He sits under the tree and leans back and **feels the soft, warm grass** against his back. He is **so relaxed, so tired,** he **can hardly keep his eyes open.**

No sooner are Moe's **eyes beginning to close** than he is dreaming. He dreams he is in the tower of a beautiful white castle. It is very tall and has white flags **floating on the breeze.** He is **so very tired** that **all he wants to do is sleep.** Moe looks for somewhere to **lie down,** where he can **just lie back and let his eyes close.**

They begin to close. He is **so tired** he needs somewhere to **fall asleep.** 'There must be a bed somewhere,' he thinks. 'I'll go down these stairs.'

Moe starts to climb down the long, winding stairs of the tower. He is **so tired** and **his feet seem so heavy** that going down the stairs is **so slow.** One step. Then another. And another.

He stops to rest. He's **yawning again.** He must continue down the stairs before **he falls asleep** for the night. So, down one more step . . . one more . . . and then down one more . . . until he comes to a beautiful room at the bottom of the stairs. **It's warm in here.** It makes Moe **feel even more like sleeping.**

Slow Moe slowly looks around the room. **It feels comfortable** in here. Very comfortable. The walls are lined with bookcases filled with books. It smells like the library at school. And it's **so quiet. He yawns again. Why is he yawning?**

He looks around the room for somewhere to lie down. Moe's **legs feel so heavy, he wants to lie down.** Against one wall of the room is an old writing desk. On it are sheets of old yellow paper with raggedy edges and an ink bottle with a feather sticking out of it. 'How strange,' thinks Slow Moe. He remembers that long ago people used to write using a feather as a pen, but he had never seen one before.

In another corner of the room is a three-legged stool barely big enough to sit on, let alone sleep on. And that's all there is. Except for a large wooden door. Where will this door take him?

Moe **yawns** and thinks, 'There is only one way to find out.'

He reaches for the big brass door knob. It doesn't move. With both hands now, he turns it. Slowly. The door begins to open. It's **very heavy.** Moe has to push hard before it moves. Slowly the door opens and Moe peers through.

All he can see is another staircase. Where does it go? He takes a step.

Down . . . step by step . . . one more . . . then one more. His **feet are getting heavier and heavier,** and **his eyes are getting heavier . . . and heavier.** Just another few steps . . .

And he is in another room. The room is bare except for large paintings on the walls. There is a painting of a beautiful lady in a long white dress with her hair flowing softly over one shoulder. **His eyes are sleepy,** but he can see she looks like his mother. Now he remembers the smell of her hair and the feel of her hands, from when she carried him as a tiny, tiny child. He is **so tired now,** he can hardly remember.

The man in the other painting looks like someone he has seen before. He has a high white collar and a black tie. On his coat is a row of shiny medals, each hanging from a colourful ribbon. As Moe looks at these medals, the man in the painting speaks. It sounds like his father's voice: 'You will find what you are looking if you keep going down the stairs.'

Moe looks around the room for stairs. But there is no door. He is **so tired he wants to lie down** and **go to sleep.** Now he notices a brass ring on the floor. **He tries not to yawn.** Why is there a ring in the floor? He takes it in his hand, turns it slowly, and a door in the floor begins to open.

It squeaks as Moe opens it. He peers through it into the dimly lit room below. All he can see is a ladder. He is **so tired now he doesn't know if he can go any further.** All he wants to do is **close his eyes and go to sleep.** But he has to try. First one step . . . then the next . . . then the next. He stops for a moment. This room is warmer than the others, and it smells familiar. He takes another step and he is here: standing at another door. **He is so tired.**

Very slowly, Moe opens the door. The room is like his own. His very own bedroom. There is a bed. It's his own bed. **It's so comfortable here. So tired.** Is this a dream? **It's so good to be in** your own bed. So you can just relax and close your eyes. After all those stairs you can feel your feet starting to relax. They are so tired. Your knees are relaxed . . . your hips . . . your tummy . . . your chest . . . your arms . . . your shoulders are relaxed . . . your neck . . . your face. And, as you drift off to a deep, relaxed sleep, you think it is a dream that you are in bed, and you are drifting off to a wonderful, relaxed sleep.

chapter four

Calmly going back to work

Children need models more

than they need critics.

Joubert

Are you going back to work?

For most parents, the big issue following the birth of your baby relates to work. In almost all developed countries, the majority of women with children under 18 are in the paid labour force. In fact, the fastest-growing labour segment is women with children under the age of six.

So, two questions inevitably arise: **Are you going back to work? If so, when?**

For many of us, financial necessity makes the first question academic. But for those who do have the luxury of being able to make the choice, there is a dilemma they must confront.

On one hand, you've just given birth to this wondrous new addition to your life, and maybe their first steps are still to come. Can you just place your child in someone else's care, even if that carer is your partner, for a large part of the day?

On the other hand, you've worked long and hard to get your career to the stage where you could think about having a baby. Can you just walk away from that and be a full-time carer?

There is enough evidence around to show that being a full-time parent or a working one should make no material difference to the way your child develops.

Try this short questionnaire to help focus your thinking.

Work or stay at home questionnaire

Go to work	Stay at home
☐ Financial independence	☐ My child under my influence only
☐ Contribute to family's finances	☐ Feel secure about his/her welfare
☐ Social interaction with adults	☐ Provide consistency in his/her life
☐ Creative use of my time	☐ One-to-one attention for him/her
☐ Recognition of my efforts	☐ Bonding
☐ Feel more capable	☐ Experience his/her love
☐ Be part of a bigger world	☐ Witness his/her growth and changes
☐ Enjoy parenting more	☐ I won't feel guilty
☐ I can always change my mind	☐ I can always change my mind

Although magazine and press articles can be very opinionated on this topic – usually reflecting the biases and justifications of the writers themselves – a significant number of studies have explored it more objectively.

My summary of these studies is that, when considering a child's behaviour, emotional wellbeing and intelligence, there doesn't seem to be much difference between children of working parents and children of non-working parents.

The factors that do make a difference tend to be more qualitative: the income and education level of the caring parent, the quality of the child care and, interestingly, the emotional state of the mother. A calm, happy mother is more likely to have a contented, well-adjusted child (all things being equal).

So the question of whether you return or work or not is more related to you and how you feel.

When?

Some parents organise their lives in such a way that childbirth is simply another activity they fit into a busy schedule. Others have to prepare well in advance.

Whether you plan to return to work within a few weeks of childbirth, or after several months, determines the type of preparation required.

If you return to work when your baby is very young, consult your child-care adviser on feeding, expressing and other procedures long before you consider placing your child in care.

Mothers who return to the workforce in the first six weeks usually have to contend with two emotional issues. The first is a cocktail of emotions resulting from the hormonal changes associated with pregnancy and childbirth; the second is guilt.

Guilt? Surely there is no reason to feel guilty.

But this feeling sometimes stems from the way women tend to view their roles. While men tend to think of career and family as being separate worlds, women are more inclined to link the two. Therefore, according to this tendency, to excel in your work world is somehow misconstrued as not paying sufficient attention to your home world. You and I can see the lack of logic in this perception, but emotions sometimes have a habit of ignoring logic.

If your return to the workforce occurs after your baby is six months or so, you will have to deal with yet another emotion: separation anxiety (pages 114–115). This occurs quite regularly in children between six and 18 months; in fact, it not only has an effect on them, but on you as well.

Leaving your baby for the first time can be heart-wrenching for many parents, especially if your child cries or clings when you try to go. You may wonder whether you're doing the right thing, whether it's too early to be leaving them like this, or whether they are emotionally ready for such a step. You might even worry, deep down, that your child will transfer their trust and affection to somebody else.

So, what are you meant to do?

The first step is to accept that your emotions and your child's reaction are not at all unusual at this stage. You might also remind yourself that quality child care satisfies your baby's need to explore and cultivate new relationships – an important part of their development, and one that can be most enriching for a child.

However, to make this transition more painless, there are a number of simple steps you can employ.

Prepare the ground

The more gradually your child is introduced to the concept of child care, the more time they will have to adjust to it.

Regardless of how skilfully you prepare, a six-month-old baby is not going to understand the subtleties of this process, nor the implications of what lies ahead. But there are levels of communication between parent and child that transcend words and superficial understanding. The fact that you discuss an issue with your child at an early stage, even when you know they don't necessarily grasp the meaning of the words you are using, helps to begin this communication.

Creating familiarity

Naturally, your baby will feel more contented and secure if they are left in a familiar environment in the care of a familiar person.

If your child isn't yet familiar with the new caregiver, it's worthwhile introducing them well in advance and, if possible, more than once. When doing this, use confident words such as, 'This is the lady who'll be showing you all these exciting new things we've been talking about. Her name's Margaret. She knows all about you and has been waiting to meet you.'

A confident tone will reassure your child that you recognise and approve of this stranger, and they will most likely mirror your reaction. There is no need to hand over your child on this first meeting – allow them to take time to warm to this newcomer.

After a few of these visits, your child should see the caregiver as a friend or acquaintance rather than someone who will be assuming the caregiving role. At this stage it is helpful to brief the caregiver thoroughly on how your child prefers to be held, what foods they like, whether they sleep with a special blanket and so on.

Once you have achieved this, it would be ideal to experiment with a few practice mini-sessions of being left in their care, just for 30 minutes or an hour.

The care environment can also be made more familiar. A couple of familiar toys, and perhaps even a photo of Mummy or Daddy, can be a comfort. Even if your baby is too young to fully appreciate exactly who is in the photograph, it becomes a useful tool for the carer. ('Look, here's Mummy. See how she's smiling? She'll be calling for you soon.')

The routine

A well-established routine creates an environment of security for a baby in child care. Your child feels calm and secure when they know what's going to happen next and that their needs will be adequately met in the meantime.

The fact that you drop your child off at a certain time each day, then collect them at the same time each day, becomes a predictable occurrence in their life. This predictability enhances your child's feelings of safety and security. You might not think someone so young would know the difference between 5 p.m. and 6 p.m., and they probably can't, but the fact that you arrive at 6 p.m. every day will quickly become an unconscious benchmark for your child to depend on.

In addition, the better defined the remainder of your child's routine, the more secure they will feel. Just as a clear-cut bedtime routine (page 111) works in getting your child ready for bed, so does the 'getting ready for the caregiver' routine.

This might begin an hour before you leave home. If your child goes to someone else's place each day, you might begin with a ritual packing of their bag. Do this in a highly visible and narrative way: 'And Teddy goes in here beside your water bottle . . . ' Even if your child can't participate in this process, they will soon begin to appreciate what is going on.

Your return

The key to your child's contentedness while you're absent is their certain knowledge that you will return. Of all the steps in the child-care process, this is the most critical.

Refer back to calm separations (pages 114–115) for tips on signposting your departures and arrivals. Consistency is the most important part of this ritual – doing it day in, day out, without fuss or embellishment. Your child will soon come to understand that when you leave them each day, you always return.

And do it with confidence. Make it obvious to your child that you feel positive about leaving them in the hands of this carer, and they will feel more confident and positive themself.

This allows no room for indecision with your goodbyes. Use your standard farewell, then leave. If you see the bleak look on your child's face then rush back to comfort them, you'll upset the ritual, which is designed to become a source of comfort for them.

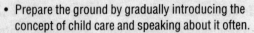

Child-care transitions

- Prepare the ground by gradually introducing the concept of child care and speaking about it often.
- Create familiarity with the caregiver and take along familiar objects.
- Establish a routine and be consistent.
- Signpost your departures and returns in a predictable way.
- Show that you are confident.

Dealing with worry

You're a new parent, you've left your child in the hands of someone else for the day, you're trying to concentrate on your work . . . but all you can think about is your baby.

Will your child be fretting without you? Will your caregiver be able to quiet them if they refuse to go to sleep? Are your caregiver's hygiene standards as pristine as your own? All these worries, and you haven't even thought about your work!

Worry Time is a simple psychological device designed to remove the sting from worrying. If you're inclined to be a 'worrier', this can be a lifesaver.

It begins with the realisation that most worries are irrational: they are based on what *might* happen rather than what *is* happening. You know from your own experience that the overwhelming majority of worries never eventuate, they don't even come close. Knowing this, of course, does not remove them. But you *can* put them into perspective with Worry Time.

Worry Time is a postponing technique. If you turn it into a habit, it becomes an effective way of diminishing worry.

All you have to do is set aside a certain period each day – the same hour is ideal – for worrying. Whether this period is 10, 30 or 60 minutes depends on how many worries you have and how prone you are to letting these colour your day. My experience is that if you start by allowing 30 minutes, you find it ends up becoming 10 minutes within a few days.

The beauty of Worry Time is that you can allow yourself to be as negative and as dramatic as you like. No-one will judge you; no-one will condemn you for it. Better still, it will not have an adverse effect on the rest of your day as long as you employ one discipline: at the end of your designated Worry Time, postpone all issues until the same time tomorrow.

During your day, every time a worrying issue arises, note it, record the details required to make a decision (if one is required), then officially postpone it until Worry Time.

When this time arrives, give your full attention to everything you've made a note of. Concentrate on these issues. Not only does this quarantine your worries from the rest of the day, but you'll be more productive in 'solving' them.

Also, there's a major side benefit: most of these concerns will have vanished or diminished before your session commences, simply because you've postponed them.

Worry Time

- Decide on a time and place for daily Worry Time.
- When a worry arises during the day, make a note of it. Forget all about it until Worry Time begins.
- At Worry Time, devote all your attention to these concerns.
- At the end of Worry Time, stop thinking about your problems entirely and fill your thoughts with other things.
- Trust in your unconscious to produce the solutions you require.

Nine times out of 10 you'll find that by the end of the day you've completely forgotten about what was worrying you.

chapter five

Calmly going it alone

The most important thing that
parents can teach their children is how
to get along without them.

Frank A. Clark

Divided responsibilities

Many parents, most of whom are women, fly solo. Often there are both emotional and economic pressures that go along with this state.

Emotionally, you may wrestle with feelings of isolation, loneliness, anxiety, guilt and over-protectiveness. This is not uncommon.

Financially, the challenges of solo parenting are equally as complex. Today, most two-parent families require two income earners and even then, many struggle to get by financially. Sole-parent families generally struggle more. Often adequate child-minding or domestic assistance is just too expensive. Many sole parents travel further to get to work, yet can afford less time to do so.

However, the burdens carried by most sole parents are not dissimilar to those experienced by two-parent families when one party combines bread-winning with child-raising. And, ironically, these pressures are not so much economic as emotional in nature.

When you have divided responsibilities – such as earning money and child-raising – you often believe you lack control over the course of your life. And, if you feel you lack control, chances are you'll be feeling stressed.

While no simple technique will overcome all of these tensions, there are ways to help alleviate many of them. These are to **decide your priorities, get help** and **keep your own time**.

Decide your priorities

When I was researching an earlier book, *Calm at Work,* I was surprised to discover there were not just two sets of tensions at play in most bread-winning/child-rearing situations – there were three.

The first two are work and home; the third pressure is a social one. What do you do with your evenings, your weekends, the rest of your life? How do you rationalise to yourself that everyone else is going to the party on Friday but you have to get home to your daughter? How do you think you'll ever get time to meet someone who'll be prepared to share your life and responsibilities?

The glib response to this is to protest that you have no time to even consider them. But for many sole parents, this third pressure is very real, and is every bit as stressful as the other two.

So, the first step in getting all these forces into perspective is to prioritise them.

This will take you 30–60 minutes. Go to a quiet place and, with nothing else on your agenda but to sit and relax, determine what are the main priorities in *your* life. Your child is probably going to be your top priority. If this is so, then the other forces (work, social) can be ranked accordingly.

Having done this, you need to *give yourself permission* to view the other interests in your life with lesser significance – at least for the time being.

If you ranked 'work' second, then assure yourself work comes second. Think through the ramifications of this. If your work really comes second, then it may not be so critical that you get a promotion this year. Or that you can't work past five on most weekdays. Or that you choose to miss a day now and then when your child is ill. Depending on your work situation, you may care to negotiate this with your employer.

To establish calm and balance in your life, you have to accept the priorities you have established. If it makes you feel better to rail against the unfairness or inequity of your predicament, go ahead – just don't wait for the world to change before making this adjustment in your thinking.

What if you ranked social interests as your second priority?

This introduces far too many challenges and possibilities to adequately address in a book of this size. However, perhaps you could join a babysitting or play group that includes solo parents of the opposite sex. Or you could choose a job where you might not set the world on fire, but where you can often meet people with interests similar to your own.

You may choose to adopt a practice called sequencing – where you pursue all you want in life, be it family, education, career or social – just not at the same time. If you make this decision, it pays to maintain contact with others from your industry, workplace or social group so that one day you can resume where you left off.

Then, in 12 months' time, it's useful to go through this exercise all over again and re-examine your priorities. Who knows, this time your child may be attending school and, with the extra time on your hands, you can make work your main priority once again.

Whichever way you turn, at least *you* are making the decisions. You are in control.

Get help

Reliable child care is much easier to write about than to find, especially if you're a sole parent. You will probably need child care throughout the day, as well as on occasions when you need to go out, or in times of difficulty.

This might mean relying on a relative, or another parent with whom you have reciprocal arrangements. It might be useful to maintain contact with other mothers and to participate in a babysitting network.

When I was in this situation myself some years ago, I advertised for a surrogate grandparent. You'd be surprised how many replies I received from un-utilised grandmothers who sought an occasional family-style involvement.

Having time to yourself is vital. Arrange a babysitter as often as you can afford so you can pursue your own interests in the evenings.

If you're separated or divorced, take full advantage of access visits – when your child visits their other parent. The better structured these arrangements, the better you can organise your own calendar to have time for yourself.

Keep your own time

As we explored in Me Time (page 19), it's vital that you set aside at least 30 minutes a day purely for your own indulgence. By doing absolutely nothing, you can escape the pressures of everyday life and rediscover the meaning of calm. Alternatively, you can spend the time meditating, relaxing or exercising when your child is asleep.

It's okay to be fanatical about this because it's not only in your interest to be fit, calm and well, it's in your child's interest as well. Just half an hour per day is all it takes.

chapter six

Calm for the rest of your life

Pretend you are calm: adopt the

characteristics of a calm person, pretend

that others see you as a calm person, and

in no time you'll be a calm person.

THE LITTLE BOOK OF CALM

Commit to being calm

There is one aspect of being a parent that's all too true: children don't remain children for long; before you know it, they've grown into adolescence and beyond.

While this book has concentrated on the first few special years of your child's life, most of the practices and techniques involved here apply throughout life.

If you've read any of my earlier books, you'll be aware of the Six Principles for Long-lasting Calm. By adopting these principles, you can virtually assure yourself of ongoing calm and contentment, no matter what life may throw your way.

The most important consideration is simply being committed to this course. If you are conscious of what you want to achieve and focus on it as something you can enjoy now, it will happen of its own accord. It is already happening.

Then, all you have to do is work towards integrating as many of the remaining five principles as you can.

Six Principles for Long-lasting Calm

1. Focus on remaining calm.
2. Meditate daily. Spend a few minutes each day sitting quietly, practising Deep Calm (pages 61–66) or something similar.
3. Look after your diet. Eat more calm foods, consume less of the foods that cause unrest (pages 43–50).
4. Exercise three times a week.
5. Maintain a positive attitude. Not only will it help you become happier and more contented, it is the key to better relationships and health.
6. Spread calm.

Can you feel it? An ongoing sense of peace and satisfaction is now within your reach.

It's yours as long as you're prepared to share. If you want to be loved, you will be loving. If you want to attract good fortune, you will share what fortune you have. If you want to be happy, you will help others to be happy.

And, above all, if you want to be calm, you will spread calm.

Just as you soothe a distressed child by speaking softly and slowly, you spread calm by endeavouring to remain calm and at ease. Demonstrably make this effort, and others will start to follow your example.

You and your children have the power to help make your world a more peaceful, caring and loving place. It is happening now. It takes so little willpower, so little effort.

All you have to do is spread calm.